CW01072929

Succeed in

Trinity

CEFR
C1

Exam Preparation & Practice Tests

ISE III Reading & Writing Module

from 2015

Andrew Betsis
Lawrence Mamas

GLOBAL ELT

Introduction to the
ISE III Reading & Writing exam

Trinity College London's Integrated Skills in English Reading & Writing ISE III exam aims to assess candidates' reading and writing skills through an integrated approach.

The texts that are included in the reading section of the exam aim to reflect the type of sources a candidate would encounter in an educational context. The types of tasks included simulate the way that candidates select and report information in an academic environment.

The writing section consists of an integrated writing task (Reading into writing) in which candidates are expected to write a response to a prompt, using information from multiple texts (one of which includes graphical information) and an independent writing task (Extended writing) in which candidates are expected to respond to a short prompt.

ISE rating scale

All tasks in each ISE level are linked to a particular CEFR level.
The rating scale below shows four distinct scores within each CEFR level:

Score	Interpretation
4	Excellent achievement - at the upper end of the CEFR level
3	Appropriate achievement - at the middle of the CEFR level
2	Acceptable achievement - of the CEFR level, possibly newly qualified at that level
1	Non-achievement - not of the CEFR level
0	Test void (e.g. paper spoiled, not attempted, illegible, unintelligible)

Published by GLOBAL ELT LTD
www.globalelt.co.uk
Copyright © **GLOBAL ELT LTD, 2015**

Linda Maria Windsor, Sean Haughton, Marianna Georgopoulou and Varvara Vallianatou have also contributed to this publication.

Every effort has been made to trace the copyright holders and we apologise in advance for any unintentional omission.
We will be happy to insert the appropriate acknowledgements in any subsequent editions.

All rights reserved. No part of this publication may be reproduced, stored in a retrieval system, or transmitted in any form or by any means, electronic, mechanical, photocopying, recording or otherwise, without the prior permission in writing of the Publisher. Any person who does any unauthorised act in relation to this publication may be liable to criminal prosecution and civil claims for damages.

British Library Cataloguing-in-Publication Data
A catalogue record of this book is available from the British Library.

● **Succeed in TRINITY ISE III - Reading & Writing - Student's Book - ISBN: 9781781642221**
● **Succeed in TRINITY ISE III - Reading & Writing - Teacher's Book - ISBN: 9781781642245**

TABLE OF CONTENTS

Task 1

Focus: **Reading Task 1**
This section will help you prepare for Reading Task 1 of the ISE III exam.

Main objective: To read a long text and answer three sets of related questions.
- Section 1: Title Matching
  (Reading for gist)
- Section 2: Selecting the True statements
  (Scanning and Careful Reading)
- Section 3: Completing Sentences
  (Scanning and Careful Reading)

Skills: **Reading for gist:** This involves reading a text fairly quickly in order to understand the general topic. You don't have to understand every single word to find out what the text is basically about.
In Section 1, you will be required to select the correct title for each of the text's five paragraphs. You will need to read each paragraph (1-5) for gist so as to understand its general topic.

Scanning: When you scan a text, you don't read every single word carefully. This is because you are looking for specific information, so not all the details of the text are important. Instead, you move down through the lines of text quickly, trying to find the information you need. When scanning, it usually helps to look for key words or ideas.

Careful reading: Sometimes, when you find the information you need by scanning, you may have to read this information slowly and carefully to make sure you get the right answer.

You may not have time in the exam to read the entire text very slowly, but you will be able to read the relevant short sections carefully to help choose the right answers.

Theme: In Reading Task 1, there are a number of different broad themes the text can be about. These include:
- Independence
- Ambitions
- Stereotypes
- Role models
- Competitiveness
- Young people's rights
- The media
- Advertising
- Lifestyles
- The arts
- The rights of the individual
- Economic issues
- Roles in the family
- Communication
- The school curriculum
- Youth behaviour
- Use of the internet
- Designer goods
- International events
- Equal opportunities
- Social issues
- The future of the planet
- Scientific developments
- Stress management

When you practise, read as many different texts as you can related to all the above themes.

Section 1: Title Matching
Pre-reading 1

Write down as many ideas as you can think of for your answers to these questions.
Then, if possible, discuss your notes with a partner.

1. Give 3 examples of how modern life benefits from technology.
2. When can technology become intrusive and what can be done about it?
3. Are there any modern technologies that we would be better without? Why?
4. In general, do you believe technology has improved our quality of life? How?
5. How do you think technology will change our lives over the next 50 years?

Exercise 1

This is **NOT** an exam task, but it will help you practise **reading for gist**. Think about how texts are structured and how the different ideas/topics are usually linked together in a logical order. When you have finished this task, you should find the actual exam task which follows easier. Why? Because Exercise 1 will help you get a general understanding of what each paragraph is about. Read the following text about *Smart toys*. The paragraphs are not in the correct order. Put the paragraphs in order from 1-5. Write the correct paragraph number on the answer line.

Reading for gist

Smart toys

Paragraph ....5..........

Possibly, Carr is worrying unduly as there is no guarantee that Google's concept will ever become reality, as is the fate of many ideas published in patents; but then again, she may not. Qualcomm has already floated the idea of a smart teddy bear in its 'house of the future' at Mobile World Congress, in Barcelona. A concept bear was able to say *'good morning'* or *'good night'* to a child in synchrony with lights being turned on or off. Indeed, as if to confirm Carr's worst fears, Mattel has already debuted Hello Barbie; a doll that taps into a Wi-Fi connection to chat with young girls and record conversations with children. The concept understandably has come under fire from critics who claim the doll's ability to record potentially sensitive information could place children at harm. Despite the maker's insistence that recorded information will remain secure and settings will be in place to permit parental control over information stored by the company's servers, many might be unwilling to buy into the idea of 'smart toys'.

Paragraph ....1........   *just an unrealistic idea*

Until now, voice-controlled toys capable of operating household appliances were a mere flight of fancy. Now, it seems, toys, modelled on animated cartoon characters, Buzz Lightyear and Woody, may soon become reality if Google's recent patent for voice-responsive Teddy and rabbit-shaped machines is approved. However, Google's voice-sensitive toys will not merely flip light switches and drive remote controlled cars, like their cartoon counterparts. In addition to controlling domestic devices like TVs, music systems and lights, they will potentially be capable of interacting with humans; not merely responding to requests, but additionally, displaying rudimentary emotions, reflecting those of the speaker.   *basic emotions*

Paragraph ....3........

Google's new toy has been trumpeted by its designers as a 'cute' home accessory and accordingly marketed in child-friendly forms which may extend to dragons, robots or even aliens to make them more compatible playmates for young children. Google suggests that by looking cute, "young children might find these forms to be attractive" and adults would be more likely to interact more naturally with them than a traditional computer interface. Homes, it suggests, could use one or a number of such toys spread around the home to facilitate family members and enable them to effortlessly perform tasks around the house. An added bonus of these toys, claims Google, is that such devices can also store conversations on the internet and would be permanently listening for instructions from homeowners to which they would respond.

Paragraph ....2........

It is envisaged that these anthropomorphic devices will be connected to the internet, responding to commands given by homeowners. Embedded in the devices will be microphones, speakers and cameras, enabling the 'toys' to respond to and execute commands relayed to them upon a simple voice command. In addition, these sophisticated gadgets will feature motors to change the toys' facial expressions. Google's patent suggests that the toy will listen for a trigger word and upon hearing it will turn to face the speaker. Using cameras, the gadget will then scan the emotional expressions of the person making eye contact with the toy. It will then respond vocally or adopt a new facial expression to exhibit surprise, for example, before carrying out domestic chores remotely, such as switching on a washing machine. According to the blurb on the patent, the device will be able "to express interest, may open its eyes, lift its head and/or focus its gaze on the user".

Paragraph ....4........

There is a fine line, however, between anthropomorphic wizardry and downright creepiness. Whilst Google might like to portray the toys as the cute toys in Disney's *Toy Story,* some believe that these anthropomorphic devices are more reminiscent of the human-like toys featured in horror and science fiction films such as Stephen Spielberg's film, '*AI*'. In the latter instance, the intelligent, 'super toy' teddy bear, capable of turning its head, talking and changing facial expressions is more beast than bear in its manipulative machinations. In fact, the unnerving capability of Google's toys to eavesdrop on conversations, store information and connect to the internet seems just one step too far for some. Emma Carr, director of surveillance monitoring group Big Brother Watch, voices her concern over privacy issues regarding such devices that record conversations and log activity. She states, "When those devices are aimed specifically at children, then for many this will step over the creep line. Children should be able to play in private and shouldn't have to fear this sort of passive invasion of their privacy. It is simply unnecessary."

Did you get the questions right? Check below. The answers are given upside down. Turn your book around to see what they are. Correct any answers you got wrong.

Paragraph: 5 - 1 - 3 - 2 - 4

Exercise 2

Now that you have completed Exercise 1, you should have a good idea what each paragraph is about. Write a short summary note of the paragraph topics in your own words on the answer lines below. Write no more than 8 words for each answer.

Paragraph 1:

....

Paragraph 2:

....

Paragraph 3:

....

Paragraph 4:

....

Paragraph 5:

....

Exercise 3

Exam-type Question Section I: Matching titles to paragraphs

This is an actual exam task. You must match each heading/title to the correct paragraph. But, be careful! There is an extra heading/title that you don't need. Sometimes the wrong answer can use words from the text to try to trick you. Read each heading/title very carefully. It may help to put the heading/title in your own words.

Questions I-5 (one mark per question)
The text on the previous page has five paragraphs (**I-5**). Choose the best title for each paragraph from **A-F** below and write the letter (**A-F**) on the lines below. There is one title you don't need.

1. Paragraph 1 ....

2. Paragraph 2 ....

3. Paragraph 3 ....

4. Paragraph 4 ....

5. Paragraph 5 ....

A Smart toy mechanisms

B Limitations of smart toys

C The future is already here

D Attractive companions

E A chilling parallel

F Products in the process of being developed

Pre-reading 2

Write down as many ideas as you can think of for your answers to these questions.
Then, if possible, discuss your notes with a partner.

1. Are forms of surveillance e.g. security cameras common in your country?

2. What are your feelings about surveillance?

3. Should children be protected from forms of surveillance? Why?/Why not?

4. Can we prevent information obtained from surveillance methods being misused, and if so, how?

5. Are there any positive aspects to surveillance?

Exercise 4

Remember: In Section I, there is always one title you don't need. Often, it will (**a**) be similar to one of the correct titles, but with a slightly different meaning, or it will (**b**) use some words from one of the paragraphs but will still be incorrect, or it will (**c**) be about an unimportant point; not the main paragraph topic.

Now, let's look at another text. This article is about *Society and surveillance*.
Read each paragraph (**I-5**) and choose the correct title (**A**, **B** or **C**).

Tip: *It is a good idea to read the main title and first few lines to get an idea of what the text is about before you start answering the questions. This will help your mind start to remember what you already know about the topic.*

IELTS 6.0

Society and Surveillance — monitoring people/activities

Paragraph 1
The majority of us stroll nonchalantly along the high street all but oblivious to the security cameras angled on city roofs and buildings, recording our every move. Maybe we would not be quite so carefree and unselfconscious if we knew that we were being caught on camera up to 300 times a day! If you take the average shopping spree as lasting for 3 hours or so, it doesn't take a mathematical genius to work out how intrusive street surveillance really is. It is not a question of a somewhat random method of surveillance in operation; there is no escaping it and it is everywhere. The UK tops the surveillance league, where an average citizen, over the course of a normal working day, is filmed covertly over 300 times.

1. **A** Ignorance is bliss   **B** Filmed at work   **C** A visible presence

Paragraph 2
Before we throw up our hands in collective horror, drawing unwelcome parallels between an Orwellian vision of the future, as portrayed in the author's dystopic world of *1984*, we should first look back to the past; as far back as the 18th century, to be exact, to see that surveillance is not merely a modern concept borne of totalitarian regimes or oppressive governments. In fact, as early as the 18th century, philosopher and social realist, Jeremy Bentham, conceived of a surveillance system capable of monitoring prisoners at all times, even if only one guard was on duty. Named the *Panopticon*, the design consisted of a central watch tower encircled by a ring of prisoners' cells, each cell being triangular in shape, so in aerial view, the prison resembled a tower surrounded by pie-like segments. Admittedly, the surveillance system (later copied in certain US prison designs, such as the 'Squirrel Cage' in Pottawattamie County and the Crawfordsville Jail, Indiana) was designed for penal correction rather than monitoring of the general public, but nevertheless this proves that surveillance is not purely a modern-day concept.

2. **A** Orwellian-inspired surveillance systems   **B** History repeats itself   **C** Surveillance as punishment

Paragraph 3
Nowadays, of course, surveillance cameras crop up everywhere and sometimes when you least expect them; secret footage of Diana, the late Princess of Wales, entering the Ladies toilet of Harvey Nichols is anecdotal. For anyone (provided they have the technological know-how or can hire a security expert to install a security camera) can set up a surveillance system either obtrusively scanning the entrance to a building, or hidden in everyday objects, such as toys or even pens, in order to permit covert filming of unsuspecting individuals. Cost, however, could be a deterrent to many would-be users, as the camera itself is only a part of the cost. Whilst a lower-end model may not set you back much, you must also be prepared to store what the camera views (tapes, CDs/DVDs, or a computer with a hard disk dedicated to the camera), in addition to software upgrades, parts, repairs and other ongoing expenses.

3. **A** The prevalence of security cameras   **B** How to set up a surveillance system   **C** How surveillance can be abused

Paragraph 4
Once installed, however, the presence of a security camera in a home or place of business can reap dividends. The obvious benefit of a surveillance camera is the security it can offer. If you aren't home or can't mind your store 24/7, the camera can record what happens in your absence. For larger properties or businesses, several surveillance cameras can be purchased to operate in a network. The view from each camera can be fed into a single control room and can also be monitored by security personnel, much akin to Benthams' central surveillance tower of the *Panopticon*.

4. **A** Monitoring systems at home   **B** A need for security personnel   **C** Surveillance when you are away

Paragraph 5
However, detractors of surveillance systems argue that security cameras merely 'record' a crime rather than prevent it. To an extent, this is true; but many criminals have at least been caught after committing a criminal offence even if the cameras did not manage to prevent the crime from being committed in the first place. A more damning criticism of surveillance cameras, however, is that they are not a) indestructible or b) always guaranteed to function. The presence of surveillance cameras is therefore rendered redundant if they fail to work. Returning to the late Princess Diana and the discussion of CCTV footage, it is telling that the last crucial moments of her life, in the Pont de l'Alma tunnel in France, were not filmed due to a malfunctioning security camera positioned in the tunnel, at the site of the crash, leading incidentally to the spawning of countless conspiracy theories claiming foul play. When it matters most, it seems, security cameras cannot always be relied upon.

5. **A** A sad irony   **B** How Princess Diana died   **C** Surveillance cameras in operation

---

Did you get the questions right? Check below. The answers are given upside down. Turn your book around to see what they are. If you had some wrong answers, find out why. Were you tricked? What tricked you?

1.A 2.B 3.A 4.C 5.A

Section 2: Selecting the True statements

Exercise I

This is **NOT** an exam task, but it will help you practise the skills you need to answer the exam-type question, which we will look at later. Remember, when answering Section 2 questions, don't read the whole text slowly and carefully – you don't have time. Scan the text to find the sections with the information you are looking for. Then, if necessary, read these short sections carefully to help you choose the right answer.

Scanning

Let's practise scanning. Look at the *Society and surveillance* article again. Identify in which paragraph there is information about each of the following. Write the correct paragraph number beside each question, **I-5**. Do this exercise as quickly as you can.

1. installing security cameras   ....
2. historical use of surveillance   ....
3. how often we are filmed by security cameras   ....
4. drawbacks of security cameras   ....
5. the purpose of security cameras   ....

Did you get the questions right? Check below. The answers are given upside down. Turn your book around to see what they are. Correct any answers you got wrong.

Paragraph 3   Paragraph 2   Paragraph 1   Paragraph 5   Paragraph 4

Exercise 2

Tip: *Use what you found out in Exercise I to help you get the answers to these questions as fast as possible.*

Decide if each statement, **I-5**, is **True** or **False**. Choose **T** (**True**) or **F** (**False**).

1. Anyone can install security cameras.   T / F
2. Bentham used surveillance systems in prisons.   T / F
3. Most people are unaware of being filmed by security cameras. T / F
4. Security cameras are a reliable substitute for security personnel. T / F
5. Security cameras can potentially provide 24-hour monitoring. T / F

Exercise 3

Tip: *Sometimes statements are neither true nor false; the information is not given in the text at all. Remember: you can only choose your answers based on the information in the text – not based on your own knowledge of the subject.*

Read **Paragraph I** again below. There are three statements about this paragraph (**I-3**). One statement is **True**, one statement is **False** and one statement is **Not Given**.

> The majority of us stroll nonchalantly along the high street all but oblivious to the security cameras angled on city roofs and buildings, recording our every move. Maybe we would not be quite so carefree and unselfconscious if we knew that we were being caught on camera up to 300 times a day! If you take the average shopping spree as lasting for 3 hours or so, it doesn't take a mathematical genius to work out how intrusive street surveillance really is. It is not a question of a somewhat random method of surveillance in operation; there is no escaping it and it is everywhere. The UK tops the surveillance league, where an average citizen, over the course of a normal working day, is filmed covertly over 300 times.

Decide which statement, **I-3**, is **True**, **False** or **Not Given**. Choose **T** (**True**), **F** (**False**) or **NG** (**Not Given**).

1. It is impossible not to be filmed when out shopping in the high street.   T / F / NG
2. The visibility of surveillance cameras makes most people self-conscious.   T / F / NG
3. Countries, other than the UK, operate different surveillance systems.   T / F / NG

Exercise 4

Now you try. Read **Paragraph 2** again below and write three statements about the information in it. One statement should be **True**, one statement should be **False** and one statement should be **Not Given**.

Before we throw up our hands in collective horror, drawing unwelcome parallels between an Orwellian vision of the future, as portrayed in the author's dystopic world of *1984*, we should first look back to the past; as far back as the 18th century, to be exact, to see that surveillance is not merely a modern concept borne of totalitarian regimes or oppressive governments. In fact, as early as the 18th century, philosopher and social realist, Jeremy Bentham, conceived of a surveillance system capable of monitoring prisoners at all times, even if only one guard was on duty. Named the *Panopticon*, the design consisted of a central watch tower encircled by a ring of prisoners' cells, each cell being triangular in shape, so in aerial view, the prison resembled a tower surrounded by pie-like segments. Admittedly, the surveillance system (later copied in certain US prison designs, such as the 'Squirrel Cage' in Pottawattamie County and the Crawfordsville Jail, Indiana) was designed for penal correction rather than monitoring of the general public, but nevertheless this proves that surveillance is not purely a modern-day concept.

1. ....
2. ....
3. ....

If possible, give your statements to a partner to answer. Then, check if they got the answers right. If not, explain why.

Exercise 5

Now look at **Paragraphs 3-5** of the article about *Society and surveillance*. Decide if each statement, **1-5**, is **True**, **False** or **Not Given**. Choose **T** (**True**), **F** (**False**) or **NG** (**Not Given**).

1. Princess Diana was unaware that she was being filmed in Harvey Nichols.   T / F / NG
2. Some security cameras are relatively cheap.   T / F / NG
3. Security cameras need to be monitored constantly.   T / F / NG
4. Surveillance cameras are better suited to large businesses.   T / F / NG
5. Crime rates have gone down since the introduction of security cameras.   T / F / NG

Exercise 6

Exam-type Question Section 2: Answering True, False or Not Given

This is an actual exam task. You don't have to decide if each statement is True, False or Not Given. Instead, you just have to select the five TRUE statements. You will have to **scan** the article to find the information that relates to each statement. You can write your answers in any order you want to. Remember: There are **three extra answers** you don't need. This means three answers are either False or Not Given.

Questions 6-10 relate to the text about *Smart toys* on pages 6-7.

Questions 6-10 (one mark per question)
Choose the five statements from **A-H** below that are TRUE according to the information given in the text on pages 6-7. Write the letters of the TRUE statements on the lines below (in any order).

6. ....

7. ....

8. ....

9. ....

10. ....

A In the past, some smart toys could mimic a range of human expressions.

B *Hello Barbie* has been received with scepticism by critics.

C Some Smart toys are capable of holding conversations.

D Parents may not believe manufacturers' claims that Smart toys are safe.

E Google's smart toys will be remotely-controlled by a special device.

F Information from Smart toys will be stored on the internet.

G Smart toys only record conversations when programmed to.

H Smart toys will be able to perform functional tasks.

Section 3: Completing Sentences

In this type of exercise, you need to select a word, phrase or number from the original text to fit in each sentence gap. You **can't change the words from the original text** – they should fit and make sense in the gaps as they are. Often, the information in the gapped sentence will be **paraphrased**. That means the gapped sentence will say the same thing as a section of the original text, but it will say it using different words. You will need to scan the original text for key words and ideas to do this task. Also, remember to check that the answer word, phrase or number you choose makes grammatical sense in the gap. If it doesn't, you've chosen the wrong option. Try again. And don't use more than the number of words stated in the question to fill each gap (usually, the maximum is three).

Exercise 1

Match the words and phrases in **Column A** to their synonyms or near-synonyms in **Column B**.

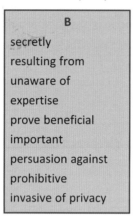

A
oblivious to
intrusive
covertly
borne of
oppressive
know-how
deterrent to
reap dividends
crucial

B
secretly
resulting from
unaware of
expertise
prove beneficial
important
persuasion against
prohibitive
invasive of privacy

Tip: *The words and phrases in Column A of this exercise are found in the second text on page 9. Choose the correct words and phrases from Column B to complete the gapped sentences in Exercise 2 below. Notice how you may not always find exactly the same words used in questions when you scan the original text. Sometimes, you will be looking for similar words or ideas.*

Exercise 2

Exam-type Question *Section 3: Completing Sentences*

Questions 11-15 (one mark per question)
Complete sentences **11-15** with a word, phrase or number from Column B (maximum three words).
Write the word, phrase or number on the lines below.

11. The average shopper is completely .... being filmed when they are out on the High Street.

12. Hidden cameras .... film their unsuspecting subjects.

13. A certain degree of .... is required to set up a security camera.

14. Sometimes surveillance cameras prove unreliable and fail to operate at .... moments.

15. A distrust of surveillance exists, ... its use by oppressive regimes.

Exercise 3

Exam-type Question *Section 3: Completing Sentences*

This is an actual exam task.
Questions 11-15 relate to the article about *Smart toys* on pages 6-7.

Questions 11-15 (one mark per question)
Complete sentences **11-15** with a word, phrase or number from the text (maximum three words).
Write the word, phrase or number on the lines below.

11. Some fear Smart toys place children .... from those who might use their personal details.

12. At the moment, Smart toys are only .... basic functions.

13. In the future, Smart toys may be able to carry out .... around the house.

14. There is a need for .... over what sites children can access on the internet.

15. Smart toys may be able to express emotions, although they will probably be ...., at best.

Task 2

Focus: Reading Task 2
This section will help you prepare for the Reading Task 2 of the ISE III exam.

Main objective: To read four short texts and answer three sets of related questions.
- Section 1: Multiple Matching
  (Reading for gist and Scanning)
- Section 2: Selecting True statements
  (Scanning and Careful Reading)
- Section 3: Completing Summary notes
  (Scanning and Careful Reading)

Skills: Reading for gist: This involves reading the four texts fairly quickly in order to understand what each one is about. You don't have to understand every single word to find out what a text is basically about.

Scanning: When you scan a text, you don't read every single word carefully. This is because you are looking for specific information, so not all the details of the text are important. Instead, you move down through the lines of text quickly, trying to find the information you need. When scanning, it usually helps to look for key words or ideas.

Careful reading: Sometimes, when you find the information you need by scanning, you may have to read this information slowly and carefully to make sure you get the right answer.

You don't have time in the exam to read all of the texts very slowly, but you will be able to read relevant short sections carefully to help choose the right answers.

Theme: In Reading Task 2, there are a number of different broad themes the texts can be about. These include:
- Independence
- Ambitions
- Stereotypes
- Role models
- Competitiveness
- Young people's rights
- The media
- Advertising
- Lifestyles
- The arts
- The rights of the individual
- Economic issues
- Roles in the family
- Communication
- The school curriculum
- Youth behaviour
- Use of the internet
- Designer goods
- International events
- Equal opportunities
- Social issues
- The future of the planet
- Scientific developments
- Stress management

When you practise, read as many different texts as you can related to all the above themes.

Section 1: Matching Information to Texts

Pre-reading

Write down as many ideas as you can think of for your answers to these questions.
Then, if possible, discuss your notes with a partner.

1. What form of communication do you use daily and why?
2. How many different forms of communication can you think of?
3. Are modern-day forms of communication better than the past? How?
4. Which method of communication, past or present, is the fastest/slowest?
5. How do you think methods of communication will evolve in the future?

Exercise 1

This is **NOT** an exam task, but it will help you practise **reading for gist**.
Read the following texts about communication. Then answer the questions, **A-D**.

Text A

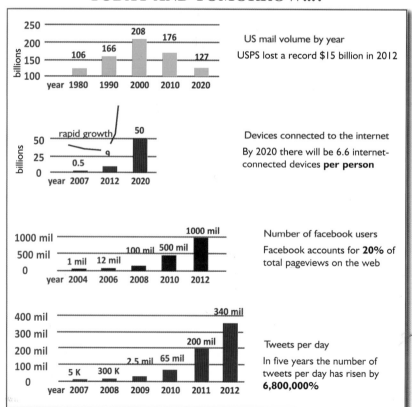

21st CENTURY COMMUNICATION:
TODAY AND TOMORROW...?

Text B

Evolution of communication

Throughout history, developments in technology and communications have gone hand-in-hand with new inventions. The latest technological developments, such as the internet and mobile devices, have taken the science of communication to an unprecedented level of efficiency.

The graphic representation of ideas or pictographs, as exemplified by the ancient Egyptian hieroglyphs, facilitated the first form of written communication. Although virtually indecipherable to the modern eye, they were instantly recognisable symbols for contemporary society at the time. Later in the 15th century, the invention of the printing press enabled the written word to be communicated over long distances rather than be committed to an unwieldy immobile slab of stone, in the case of hieroglyphs.

Finally, the most groundbreaking invention to date, that of the internet, permitted instant written and verbal communication over long distances. 20th century methods of written communication, such as telegrams and letters, have been rendered virtually obsolete in the 21st century by internet communication which is vastly more efficient and also cost effective. E-mails and instant messaging obviate the need to wait hours in post office queues and also the need to buy stamps for letters. They also arrive instantly in the recipient's e-mail box or account, so there is no waiting on an unreliable postal service to relay information.

Text C

From: Jack Saunders
To: Lorna Brinksworth
Subject: Re: information for school project

Dear Lorna,
You told me you are doing a school project on the use of mobiles and their effect on society. Well, I have set out a few notes for you below to aid you with your research.

- Mobile phones permit high quality communication worldwide at a comparatively low cost.
- Increasing prevalence of mobile phones has precipitated a marked decline in face-to-face communications.
- The increased prevalence of mobile phones, has seen an increased reliance on verbal and written communication over electronic mediums such as e-mail.
- Small keyboards on mobile phones have resulted in the radical shortening of words with little or no adherence to traditional grammatical rules.
- Communication has become concise and short.
- Use of 'emoticons' has become widespread to counter the negative effect of brevity in communication being seen as abrupt or rude.
- Although nowadays communications are shorter, the volume of communications has increased dramatically due to the ease with which mobile phones can communicate information.

So, I hope that will help you. Much as I welcome new technology I do miss the old-fashioned methods of communication, like letter-writing. However, as you see, I'm replying to you by e-mail as it's so much faster than a letter so I guess we have to move with the times!

All the best,
Jack

Text D

Dear parents,

I am aware that many pupils at Downton High School regularly use mobile phones. Whilst mobiles serve multiple purposes, enabling instant access to information, communication with friends and allowing the mobilisation of emergency services if necessary, I feel compelled to rule against their use in school.

Recent scientific research has proven unequivocally that cell phone radiation damages children's brains. Those most vulnerable are pre-teens, as they are particularly sensitive to the effects of cell phone radiation. It seems irresponsible therefore to expose young children to such a hazard.

However, my chief concern, since I am responsible for the educational development of pupils at Downton High, is the disruption to lessons caused by mobiles. Although teachers try to enforce the 'no mobiles in lessons' rule, many pupils blatantly disregard school ruling. Confiscating phones used in lessons has been to no avail. Therefore, I have taken the decision to ban all mobiles whilst on school property.

I know that this ban may prove unpalatable to some but I am acting entirely in the interests of the pupils by prohibiting mobiles in school. I hope that you will help enforce the ban by ensuring your child does not take a mobile with them to school.

Thank you in advance for your co-operation.

Yours faithfully,
Marjorie Branning

A. Match the descriptions to the texts (**A-D**). Write **A**, **B**, **C** or **D** on the answer line.

1. This text compares current and projected usage of communications.   Text ....

2. This text is an opinion text expressing intolerance of a form of communication.   Text ....

3. This text is an unbiased account of the impact of a type of communication.   Text ....

4. This text relates the development of communication to specific events.   Text ....

B. In which text would you find information about:

1. how society has been changed by a type of communication   Text ....

2. the interaction of historical events and advances in communication   Text ....

3. reasons why a form of communication is unacceptable/hazardous   Text ....

4. how popular social networking sites will be in the future   Text ....

C. Match the alternative titles to the texts (**A-D**). Write **A**, **B**, **C** or **D** on the answer line.

1. The far-reaching effects of one form of communication   Text ....

2. Anticipated changes in communications   Text ....

3. When communication hinders rather than helps   Text ....

4. How communication never develops in isolation   Text ....

*Now, before doing question **D**, check if your answers for questions **A-C** were right. If you got any wrong, read the text(s) carefully to help you understand why, or ask your teacher for help.*

D. Now, in your own words, write a short, general summary of each text below.

Text A: ....

....

Text B: ....

....

Text C: ....

....

Text D: ....

....

Exercise 2
Exam-type Question Section 1: Matching information to texts

This is an actual exam task. You must match each piece of information to the correct text. Remember: there are five questions and only four texts. The same text can be the answer for up to two questions.

Now that you have finished Exercise 1, you should have a good idea what each text is about, which will hopefully make the questions easier to complete (because you will know where to look for the answers). It is often helpful to summarise each text in your own words once you've read it (as we did in question **D** of Exercise 1). You don't actually have to write down the summary; just think of a short one and say it to yourself – it's quicker.

Questions 16-20 (one mark per question)
Read questions **16-20** first and then read texts **A**, **B**, **C** and **D**. As you read each text, decide which text each question refers to. Choose one letter – **A**, **B**, **C** or **D** – and write it on the lines below. You can use any letter more than once.

Which text:

16. calls for united action against a method of communication?   Text ....

17. refers to the physical limitations of a modern method of communication? Text ....

18. illustrates the comparative popularity of certain social networking sites?   Text ....

19. refers to the progress of communication as an interactive process?   Text ....

20. voices an opinion over the progress of communication?   Text ....

When you completed Exercise 2, did you notice you had to use two different reading skills – **reading for gist** and **scanning**? Section 1 questions mainly require you to understand the general topic, but one or two questions can also be about specific details. Remember, when scanning, if you find the piece of information you think is correct, read it carefully to make sure.

Reading 2

Text A

Since mobile phones revolutionised communication nearly 2 decades ago, 35,000 masts and base stations have cropped up all over Britain. With 3 out of 4 people owning a mobile phone along with the rapid advancements in phone technology, this figure could be set to double.

There have always been objections to the erection of phone masts, not least because of their unsightly bulk. Many residents, living, quite literally, in the shadow of a mast are concerned too with the potential risk such masts pose to their health.

Circumstantial evidence gathered from residents living close to masts indicate a higher than normal prevalence of nosebleeds and headaches amongst the population studied. It has been suggested that the siting of mobile phone masts near residential areas can lead to increased cancer rates. However, no statistical evidence exists to suggest a definite link between cancer and prolonged close contact to phone masts.

Due to the controversial nature of the siting of mobile phone masts, mobile phone companies have a policy of inviting local comment before the erection of a mast near a residential area. It is normal practice to alert residents to the potential siting of a mast and to provide information in the form of photographs and plans at local town halls. Should substantial objections be raised to the projected plans for a mast, then re-siting of the mast will be considered and an alternative site will be found.

Text B

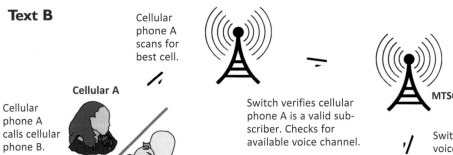

Cellular phone A scans for best cell.

Cellular A

Cellular phone A calls cellular phone B.

Cellular B

Switch verifies cellular phone A is a valid subscriber. Checks for available voice channel.

MTSO

Switch verifies 'B' is a valid subscriber. Verifies voice channel for 'B'. Checks no features active. Checks both cellular phones to voice channels and establishes voice path. Monitors both phones during call for hand off requirements or release.

Locates cellular phone B's strongest cell.

Scans for cellular phone B globally.

Text C

A large mobile phone mast is being proposed for a mainly residential area of Staunton Village. Council planners are being asked to approve an application for the replacement of the existing 14.3m pole on Maidvale Avenue with a 15m pole supporting three antennas, plus two additional equipment cabinets at ground level.

Telecom has told the local authority: "As part of Tiviphonica's and Vocalfone's continued network improvement pro-gramme, there is a specific requirement for a radio base station at this location to provide continued and enhanced 3G coverage and new 4G coverage to the surrounding areas."

Plans for the siting of the mast will be displayed in Ridgeway School on Greenfield Avenue from the beginning of next month. All local residents are encouraged to view the plans, which will affect those living in the vicinity of the Cauldwell Housing Estate. Proposals for any amendments may be made to the local council. If plans are approved, it is envisaged that the mast will be erected as early as this coming autumn.

Text D

The Government will invest up to £150 million to improve mobile coverage in the UK, the Chancellor announced today. It will aim to extend mobile service coverage to 99 per cent of the UK population. This long over-due investment will improve the coverage and quality of mobile services for the 5 to 10 per cent of consumers and businesses that live and work in areas of the UK where existing mobile coverage is poor or non-existent. Improved mobile phone communications will greatly improve the quality of life for both residents and local businesses. Residents, such as the elderly and vulnerable, will benefit especially from the reassurance of being able to keep in touch with the local community, whilst businesses will have round-the-clock network coverage, ensuring the smooth running of operations. The unprecedented coverage is likely to prove universally popular. Whilst objections to mobile phone masts have been raised in the past, they are now recognised as a possibly unwelcome but indispensable part of modern life.

A closer look at timings

The Reading and Writing exam lasts for two hours. Here is how it is recommended that you divide your time:

Task 1 (Long reading – single text and 15 related questions: 1-15)	20 minutes
Task 2 (Multi-text reading – four short texts and 15 related questions: 16-30)	20 minutes
Task 3 (Reading into writing)	40 minutes
Task 4 (Extended writing)	40 minutes

As you can see from this table, you don't have a lot of time to do the Reading questions. We recommend doing some or all of the practice tests in this book **under exam conditions** so that you can get used to answering the questions quickly. This will also help you improve your skimming and scanning skills.

When we practise at home or in class, we often allow ourselves more time to find the correct answers to the questions and ensure we understand them fully. In other words, we end up doing a lot of *careful reading* instead of *skimming* and *scanning*. However, in the exam, there may not be enough time for this. By practising under exam conditions, you will force yourself to improve your skimming and scanning skills and make them more effective.

You can always go back and do the questions again later if you want to better, or, more fully, understand what the texts are about, but do attempt them in real exam conditions first.

Section 2: **Selecting the True statements**

This is similar to Section 2 in Reading Task 1, which we already looked at. Again, your task is to choose only the FIVE TRUE statements from the eight statements given. That means there are three false statements. Remember: You can list your answers **in any order**.

Exercise 1

Let's continue to practise under exam conditions. You've already spent ten minutes reading the four texts, so you should now be familiar with the general topic of each text and the kind of information that there is in each one. Allow yourself FIVE MINUTES to complete this next exam task.

Exam-type Question Section 2: Answering True or False
This is an actual exam task.
Questions 21-25 relate to the texts about *Mobile phone masts* on pages 17-18.

Questions 21-25 (one mark per question)
Choose the five statements from **A-H** below that are TRUE according to the information given in the text on pages 17-18. Write the letters of the TRUE statements on the lines below (in any order).

21.	A	The proposal for a mobile mast in Staunton Village is a response to local demand.
22.	B	The mobile mast planned for Staunton Village will be more visible than the previous one.
23.	C	Calls between cellular phones are monitored to facilitate certain user functions.
24.	D	Most residents are indifferent to the mobile phone masts in their areas.
25.	E	There is no definite proof that living close to phone masts adversely affects health.
	F	Before the erection of a phone mast, local residents are consulted.
	G	Increased mobile phone coverage will benefit up to 10% of the UK population
	H	Improved mobile phone coverage will improve efficiency of local businesses.

Scanning

Look at Exercise 1 above and think about how you can quickly scan the texts to find the information you need. For example, Statements A and B are about *Staunton Village*. You can scan the four texts quickly to find where this term appears. Then read the short section carefully. You don't need to read all four texts again to find the answer.

Similarly, statements D and E mention health concerns related to *mobile masts*. If you scan where this topic is mentioned, you will find it in Text A in paragraphs 1 and 2.

Statements G and H refer to mobile coverage. Scanning the texts will reveal that this term is referred to in Text D.

This is what scanning is all about – quickly finding the section of the text where the answer is. You can then read this short section carefully, if necessary, to confirm your answer.

Exercise 2

Careful reading
Sometimes, after you scan the texts and find the information you need, it is necessary to read that information carefully to make sure you understand it and choose the correct answer. Statements that look similar can sometimes mean very different things. To show you what we mean by this, let's do another True or False exercise that will require careful reading.

Read these short sections (**1-6**) from the texts about *Mobile phone masts* again carefully. Then choose the true statement (**A, B** or **C**).

1. Since mobile phones revolutionised communication nearly 2 decades ago, 35,000 masts and base stations have cropped up all over Britain. With 3 out of 4 people owning a mobile phone along with the rapid advancements in phone technology, this figure could be set to double.

   A Twice as many people will own mobile phones in the future.
   B There will be twice the demand for mobile phones in the future.
   C Twice as many phone masts as already exist are projected for the future.

2. Due to the controversial nature of the siting of mobile phone masts, mobile phone companies have a policy of inviting local comment before the erection of a mast near a residential area. It is normal practice to alert residents to the potential siting of a mast and to provide information in the form of photographs and plans at local town halls.

   A Mobile phone companies consult local authorities over siting of phone masts.
   B The projected siting of a phone mast is only publicised by mobile phone companies under certain circumstances.
   C It is standard policy of mobile phone companies to alert local authorities whenever a phone mast is to be erected.

3. Switch verifies 'B' is a valid subscriber. Verifies voice channel for 'B'. Checks no features active. Checks both cellular phones to voice channels and establishes voice path. Monitors both phones during call for hands off requirements or release.

A　Mobile phone 'B' must be initially inactive to receive calls.

B　The main function of the switch is to monitor mobile phone 'B' during the call.

C　Mobile phone 'B' automatically connects to caller without the use of the switch.

4. Plans for the siting of the mast will be displayed in Ridgeway School on Greenfield Avenue from the beginning of next month. All local residents are encouraged to view the plans, which will affect those living in the vicinity of the Cauldwell Housing Estate. Proposals for any amendments may be made to the local council. If plans are approved, it is envisaged that the mast will be erected as early as this coming autumn.

A　The local council will decide on the positioning of the phone mast.

B　It is proposed that the phone mast will be positioned near Ridgeway school.

C　Plans are for the phone mast to be erected in a residential area.

5. The Government will invest up to £150 million to improve mobile coverage in the UK, the Chancellor announced today. The Government will aim to extend mobile service coverage to 99 per cent of the UK population.
This long over-due investment will improve the coverage and quality of mobile services for the 5 to 10 per cent of consumers and businesses that live and work in areas of the UK where existing mobile coverage is poor or non-existent.

A　Financial support from the government for mobile phone services has been slow.

B　Government response to public demand for improved mobile phone coverage was swift.

C　Government investment in improved mobile phone services will be delayed.

6. The unprecedented coverage is likely to prove universally popular. Whilst objections to mobile phone masts have been raised in the past, they are now recognised as a possibly unwelcome, but indispensable, part of modern life.

A　Public opinion of mobile phone masts is likely to change.

B　Public objection to mobile phone masts is likely to continue.

C　Public opinion of mobile phone masts has now changed.

Careful reading
Now that you have done Exercise 2, you should understand why careful reading is often necessary to get the right answer. Often, false statements will use words or phrases from the original texts to try to trick you. Or they can be very close in meaning but not exactly the same as the true statements. Read carefully if you're not sure.

Timing
Now let's practise the skills of scanning and careful reading again, under exam conditions. Allow yourself FIVE MINUTES to complete this next exam task.

Exercise 3

Exam-type Question Section 2: Answering True or False
This is an actual exam task.
Questions 21-25 relate to the texts about *Communication* on pages 14-16.

Questions 21-25 (one mark per question)
Choose the five statements from **A-H** below that are TRUE according to the information given in the text on pages 14-16.
Write the letters of the TRUE statements on the lines below (in any order).

	A	2012 saw the most significant losses ever in the US postal system.
21.	B	In 2012, Facebook was nearly 3 times more popular than Twitter.
22.	C	Communication by pictographs became unpopular when easier letters were introduced.
23.	D	Mobile phones facilitate face-to-face contact.
24.	E	Insufficient knowledge of grammar leads to mobile texts having errors.
25.	F	Younger children are more sensitive to mobile phone radiation than older children.
	G	Downton High school is attempting to prohibit mobile phone use in school.
	H	Previous rulings over mobile phones have proved ineffective at Downton High School.

Section 3: Summary Notes Completion

In this type of exercise, you need to select a word, phrase or number from the original text to fit in each sentence gap.
You **can't change the words from the original text** – they should fit and make sense in the gaps as they are. Often, the information in the gapped notes will be **paraphrased**. That means the gapped sentence will say the same thing in summary form as a section of the original text, but it will say it using different words or abbreviations (short forms, e.g. **info,** instead of **information**, etc.). You will need to scan the original text for key words and ideas to do this task.

Also, remember to check that the answer word, phrase or number you choose makes grammatical sense in the gap. If it doesn't, you've chosen the wrong option. Try again. And don't use more than the number of words stated in the question to fill each gap (usually, the maximum is three).

Exercise 1

Match the words and phrases in **Column A** to their antonyms or near-antonyms in **Column B**.
(*An antonym means the* **opposite** *of another word.*)

A		B	
unwieldy	vulnerable	portable	conservative
radical	risen	in use	departure from
obsolete	adherence to	decreased	protected

Tip: *The words and phrases in Column A of this exercise are found in the original texts about Communication. The words and phrases in Column B are found in the gapped sentences in Exercise 2**C**. This exercise should help you complete Exercise 2**B**.*

Exercise 2

A. Read the texts about *Communication* on pages 14-16 again. Match the texts (**A-D**) to the general topics (**1-4**).

1. Improvement of communications over time   Text ....
2. A need for a new approach to a form of communication   Text ....
3. The changing face of modern communications   Text ....
4. The impact of mobile phones on society   Text ....

B. Read statements **A-F** and match each statement to the correct topic from **A** (**1-4**). Write the correct topic number at the end of each statement. (*Don't worry about the gaps for now.*)

A. There are concerns that young children are not adequately .... from mobile phone radiation.   _____

B. Early forms of writing, like hieroglyphs, were not in a .... format.   _____

C. Many forms of communication, like the US postal service, are barely .... any more.   _____

D. Text messaging has challenged more .... grammar rules.   _____

E. The volume of US mail has .... significantly in recent years.   _____

F. The popularity of text messaging has led to a .... rules of traditional writing.   _____

What have you done in **A** and **B** of this Exercise? Think about it. **A** asked you to **match** the **topics** to the **texts**. That means you needed to understand the general topic: gist reading. This is what you do for Section 1 (*Matching Info to Texts*) questions.

B asked you to **match** the **statements** to where you're likely to find them in the **texts**. And this is basically what you do first when tackling Section 2 (*True or False*) and Section 3 (*Summary Notes Completion*) questions.

So, in Section 1 you mainly **read for gist**. Use what you learn about the texts' general topics in Section 1 to help you predict where to find the information you need for Section 2 and Section 3 questions. Then **scan** the relevant section to find each answer quickly. **Read** this information **carefully**, if necessary, to confirm. This is basically your exam strategy. Use what you learn from doing each set of questions for the next set.

C.
Now that you have identified where in the texts you will probably find the information you need, complete the gaps in sentences **A-F** in **B**. Use between one and three words from the texts in each gap.

Exercise 3

Exam-type Question Section 3: Summary Notes Completion
This is an actual exam task.
Questions 26-30 relate to the texts about *Communication* on pages 14-16.

Questions 26-30 (one mark per question)
The summary notes below contain information from the texts on pages 14-16. Find a word or phrase from texts **A-D** to complete the missing information in gaps 26-30. Write your answers on the lines below.

Summary Notes

Communication past and present

Historical uses of communication:

- advances in communication occurred alongside inventions
- early forms of communication, **(26.)**.. Egyptian hieroglyphs - pictorial
- hieroglyphic writings - of limited use, not portable
- advent of **(27.)**.. enabled freer circulation of the written word
- 20th century: internet revolutionised worldwide communication
- mobile phones - instant worldwide communication

Impact of the mobile phone:

- decrease in **(28.)**.................................... contact
- changes in written communications
- increase in the **(29.)**.................................... texts sent
- major drawback: cell phone radiation
- disruptive influence in school lessons

How communications will change in the future:

- **(30.)**.. in use of internet-connected devices by 2020
- increased popularity of social networking sites
- dramatic reduction in US postal services usage

Exercise 4

Exam-type Question *Section 3: Summary Notes Completion*
This is an actual exam task.
Questions 26-30 relate to the texts about *Mobile phone masts* on pages 17-18.

Questions 26-30 (one mark per question)

The summary notes below contain information from the texts on pages 17-18. Find a word or phrase from texts **A-D** to complete the missing information in gaps 26-30. Write your answers on the lines below.

Summary Notes

Mobile phone masts

Where they are/what they do:

- mobile masts all over Britain
- often placed near **(26.)**..
- masts ensure adequate mobile service coverage
- when connected, a mobile phone **(27.)**.................................... the mast emitting the strongest signal

Potential problems:

- headaches and nosebleeds
- the **(28.)**... of mobile masts can ruin a landscape

Benefits of mobile phone masts:

- improved mobile service coverage - the elderly remain **(29.)**.......................... with the rest of society
- better operations of businesses

Mobile phone masts in the future:

- today they are **(30.)**... to communications - likely to remain around
- up to £150 million investment planned by UK government

Task 3

Focus:
Reading into writing Task 3
This section will help you prepare for Task 3 of the ISE III exam, Reading into writing.

Main objective:
To practise the five possible kinds of Writing task in this section.

- descriptive essay
- discursive essay
- argumentative essay
- report
- article

In Task 3, you must produce a written answer using relevant information selected from the four texts in Reading Task 2.

Question types:

(1) Essay

- use a formal or neutral register
- use full forms *(e.g. **cannot** not **can't**)*

Descriptive essay: This type of essay involves writing a description of something, e.g. 'a day in the life of a dairy farmer' or presenting factual information about something, e.g. 'how to make glass'. It normally looks like this:

Use the information from the four texts you read in Task 2 to write an essay (200-230 words) for ...

Discursive essay: This type of essay involves discussing a topic, e.g. 'how to make our city streets safer' or 'the advantages and disadvantages of renewable power'. You either need to evaluate some options and present a balanced point of view or examine different solutions to a problem and then give your view at the end. It normally looks like this:

Use the information from the four texts you read in Task 2 to write an essay (200-230 words) for ... looking at ways to solve the problem of ....

Argumentative essay: This type of essay involves deciding if you agree, disagree or neither agree nor disagree with a statement, e.g. 'Team sports are more fun than individual sports'. You should examine the topic carefully, make your opinion clear and support it. You can agree or disagree strongly, so long as you explain why. It normally looks like this:

Use the information from the four texts you read in Task 2 to write an essay (200-230 words) about the following topic: ....

(2) Report

- use a formal register
- give the report a title and give each section a heading
- use full forms (e.g. *is not* not *isn't*)

Report: In a report, you will (a) state the issue that you are examining, then (b) discuss the facts or information you have and finally (c) give your conclusions/recommendations. It normally looks like this:

Use the information from the four texts you read in Task 2 to write a report (200-230 words) for ....

(3) Article

- use an informal register
- give the article a main title or heading
- use contractions (e.g. *can't* not *cannot*)
- use colourful language to make your answer interesting and catch the reader's attention

Article: The types of articles you may have to do are similar to the three types of essays. You may have to (1) describe something, (2) discuss something or (3) argue something. The difference between an article and an essay is that articles are usually written in a less formal style. You want to make your writing as interesting as possible. It normally looks like this:

Use the information from the four texts you read in Task 2 to write an article (200-230 words) for your .... about ....

Using titles and headings
It is important to know about the format of different types of writing. Generally speaking, in an essay, you don't need to use a main title or subheadings for each paragraph. In a report you should use both a main title and paragraph headings. In an article, you should use a main title but not paragraph headings.

Descriptive Essay
Pre-reading

Write down as many ideas as you can think of for your answers to these questions. Then, if possible, discuss your notes with a partner.

1. How often and when do you speak English?

2. Is it better to have one global language? Why?/Why not?

3. Do you think that English should be the No.1 language? Why?/Why not?

4. In your opinion, will English continue to be the No.1 language? Why?/Why not?

5. For what reasons do you think English evolved to be the No.1 language?

Exercise 1

Remember, in the exam, you will do Reading Task 2 before Reading into writing Task 3. You will, therefore, already be familiar with the texts connected with Task 3 and what they are about because the texts are from Reading Task 2. Use what you already know from doing Task 2 to your advantage when finding the information you need for Task 3.

Read the texts about the *English Language* below. Try to get a gist or general understanding of what they are about. Then answer the questions. Match the topics (1-4) to the texts. Write **A**, **B**, **C** or **D** on the answer lines.

1. The roots of the English language　　　　　　　Text ....

2. Specific reasons to learn English　　　　　　　Text ....

3. A need for a new global language　　　　　　　Text ....

4. How English became global and its role now and in the future　　　Text ....

Text A

The rise to dominance as a global language

With the rise of British colonialism, English became the language of choice for the colonies of the British Empire. In the post-colonial period, many of the English-speaking newly created nations, which had multiple indigenous languages, opted to continue using English as the lingua franca to avoid the political difficulties inherent in promoting one indigenous language over another. Since the British Empire spanned the globe from North America to India, Africa, Australia and New Zealand, by the late 19th century, English had become a truly global language. In the latter half of the 20th century, widespread use of English was further reinforced by the global economic, financial, scientific, military and cultural pre-eminence of the English-speaking countries, especially the USA. Today English is the most widely spoken language in the world, with speakers of the English language totalling around 1.8 billion. It is also the most widely-taught language worldwide and used in virtually every field conceivable, from shipping and medicine to education and computing, as the lingua franca.

What the future holds for English though, is uncertain. The economic dominance of English-speaking countries is being eroded as Asian economies are growing. Asian countries are now the source, not the recipient, of cultural and economic flows. Additionally, the population of rich countries is ageing as the young with disposable income are increasingly those from Asia and Latin America, rather than the USA. A possible future decline in the prominence of the English language is indicated in a sea change in school curricula. In Australia, Chinese is now the second language taught in schools and this may just be the beginning of a linguistic trend in future education. The period of most rapid change, which seems imminent, is likely to last about 20 years and will be a critical time for the English language and those dependent on it.

Text B

Communicate in English

We are offering courses in English this summer at our High Wickham College in Oxfordshire. Due to the popularity of this course, places are limited, so if you're thinking of improving your English, don't hesitate, sign up now. If you are still undecided, we've set out a list of reasons why you should learn English, below:

- An estimated 85% of scientific articles are written in English. So if you want to study science and technology, English is a prerequisite.

- Everyone uses the internet today but did you know 55% of the world's webpages are written in English? So, without a basic knowledge of English, you will be denying yourself access to a wealth of information on the internet.

- Major sporting events, such as the Olympics, are held in English, as are many international conferences. Therefore, if you envisage a career that will necessitate your attending conferences, learning English will be of enormous benefit to you in years to come.

- With increasing globalisation, international travel is now the norm. Knowing English will stand you in good stead, in allowing you to survive in foreign, English-speaking countries.

- Being fluent in a second language demonstrates someone with intellect and commitment. If you can add a complex language, like English, to your CV then you will be ahead in the job market.

- Finally, a knowledge of English can allow you to get more from popular culture. The world's highest-grossing movies are made in Hollywood and therefore are in English. Moreover, most pop songs that become international hits, invariably have English lyrics. So, kiss those annoying cinema subtitles goodbye and get more out of the music you enjoy by learning English.

So, what are you waiting for? Sign up now to our summer course and a wealth of opportunities will open up for you!
Enquiries should be made to: The Principal, High Wickham College, Ruislip Rd, Oxfordshire (Tel: 07672 7689000)

Text C

Dear Editor,

Like countless other people, I experience the continual frustration of going abroad and not being able to communicate. Whilst English is supposedly the No.1 language, quite frankly in some countries, you wouldn't think it. Even in good hotels, the receptionists often speak basic or broken English.

I believe the solution is to make Esperanto the global language. After all, Esperanto was created with simplicity in mind. All complex grammar rules and difficult vocabulary are absent in this wonderfully easy and expressive language.

If we all learnt Esperanto at school then global communication would become so much simpler than it is today. English may be the lingua franca today, but how many people actually speak it at a proficient level? A language like Esperanto, on the other hand, would be accessible to everyone: linguists and non-linguists alike.

I think we have given English a fair trial as a global language and seen that few can achieve the level of linguistic competence necessary for it to be considered the No.1 language. Now is the time for change and in response to increasing globalisation to adopt the more accessible language of Esperanto.

Yours faithfully,
J. Saunders

Text D

Linguistic origins of the English language

- Germanic languages, as well as French and Latin, have exerted the most influence on English language development.

- French, Latin and Germanic languages have exerted an approximately equal influence on the English language.

- The total influence exerted by Greek, proper names and unspecified languages is slightly less than that exerted by the single influence of either Latin, French or Germanic languages.

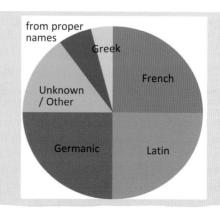

Exercise 2

Before doing the next exercise, check your answers to Exercise 1.

Now let's look at the actual Task 3 question: *Use the information from the four texts you read in Task 2 (pages 25-26) to write an essay (200-230 words) for your teacher describing the role of English today and in the future.*

Please bear in mind that in the actual exam candidates are expected to use information from all four texts. However, for the purposes of this book task we will concentrate on just two texts.

Decide which two texts, **A-D**, have information you will need to answer this question. Remember, the essay is about the role played by English today and in the future; not about its origins, complexity or its accessibility as a global language.
Tick (✔) the texts you think are relevant.

1. Text A ☐   2. Text B ☐   3. Text C ☐   4. Text D ☐

Exercise 3

Before doing the next exercise, check your answers to Exercise 2.

Now that you have decided where you can find the information that you need in order to answer the question, think about HOW you are going to answer it. In the exam, your writing is marked on the following:

- **Task fulfilment**
  o Did you answer the question and did you use appropriate information from the texts to do this?
  o Did you organise your ideas into paragraphs, with an introduction, main body paragraphs and a conclusion?
  o Did you link your ideas together in a logical way and is your answer easy to follow?
  o Did you use the correct style of writing, e.g. *formal* and *with a title* and *headings* for a **report**?
  o Did the text have a positive effect on the reader?

- **Accuracy and range**
  o Did you use a range of different grammatical functions accurately to express yourself?
  o Did you use a wide range of vocabulary?
  o Did you use accurate spelling and punctuation?

A. Planning is key to writing a good answer. Put the information in your essay in the right order. Write the correct paragraph number (e.g. 1, 2, 3, or 4) on the answer line.

A. Examples of how English is used in virtually every aspect of life
   e.g. from work to the Internet and popular culture.   Paragraph ....

B. A brief summary of what you have said.   Paragraph ....

C. A general introduction describing the present status of the English language
   and indicating its future role e.g. % of English speakers worldwide, overview
   of its widespread use, future predictions.   Paragraph ....

D. The future of English as a global language, predictions, changes underway
   - ageing population, school curricula, decline of English-speaking countries,
   rise of Asian economy.   Paragraph ....

*Check your answers to Question **A** before continuing.*

B. Now match the information (i-iii) to the text you will find it in (**A-D**). Write **A**, **B**, **C** or **D** on the answer lines.

i. A general introduction describing how English is the global language as defined by
   the number of English speakers, worldwide and its universal acceptance.   Text ....

ii. Specific usages of the English language in every aspect of life.   Text ....

iii. Information about the future role of English, shift in population demographics and
   world economy, changes in school curricula.   Text ....

*Check your answers to Question **B** before continuing.*

Note: Sometimes, the information you will need for a single paragraph will be found in more than one text.

C. The first step is to decide what you want to say in each paragraph. The next step is to decide where in the texts you will find this information. We have already done this in the questions **A** and **B**.

Now, the next step is to start making some notes for specifically what to write in each paragraph. To do this, you have to pick out the key information from the texts.

Text A contains the information you need for your first paragraph, the introduction. Tick [✓] the important points we should use to describe the current and future status of the English language.

A. Why English was chosen as a global language ☐

B. The prevalence of English up until the 20th century ☐

C. Current total of English speakers worldwide ☐

D. Countries where English is spoken today ☐

E. English as the most widely-taught language worldwide ☐

F. Overview of areas where English is used e.g. computing, medicine ☐

G. Predicted economic and demographic changes ☐

H. How far the British Empire used to extend ☐

D. Now make notes on the information you need for **Paragraph 2** and **Paragraph 3**. Remember in which of the original texts you found each piece of key information (*see answers to Question B*).

Paragraph 2 (Examples of how English is used in virtually every aspect of life e.g. from work to the Internet and popular culture)
....
....

Paragraph 3 (What factors will affect the role of English in the future e.g. economic and demographic changes)
....
....

E. Now you have the information you need to make a complete plan of your essay. Complete your plan below.

Paragraph 1
....
....

Paragraph 2
....
....

Paragraph 3
....
....

Paragraph 4
....
....

Planning

You have now finished planning. Think about the steps you took. Use these steps each time you plan a Task 3 question.

Step 1: Think about what you want to say in each paragraph, then decide and write down your paragraph topics.

Step 2: Think about where you will find the information you need for each paragraph in the original texts. Match the texts to your paragraphs.

Step 3: Take note of key points from the text to use in your paragraphs.

Step 4: Prepare your finished plan.

Writing your answer - paraphrase

Add textual content: You should not repeat the information in the original texts using the same words in your answer. You must **paraphrase** (use a different way of saying things). Basically, put the information in the original texts into **your own words**. The same rule applies to titles and headings – never copy these from the original text.

Exercise 4

In this exercise, you will practise paraphrasing information.
Let's have a look at the example plan for the first paragraph and an example answer.

Example plan
Paragraph 1

- globalisation - English No.1 language
- 1.8 billion English speakers worldwide
- English spoken over 5 continents (America, Asia, Australia, Europe, Africa)
- English most widely taught language
- widespread use of English – variety of sectors
- future of English, its projected decline as populations age, shift in world economy
- predicted rise of Asian languages

Example answer

With increasing globalisation, English has risen to global prominence. It is now ranked in top place amongst languages worldwide. Currently, 1.8 billion people speak English over the world. Their countries of origin span the globe, taking in 5 continents from America to Asia and Australia. Not surprisingly, English is the most popular language to learn. There is a constant demand to learn the language which is the lingua franca today in a wide range of fields from medicine to computing. How long English will remain secure in its position as the No.1 language will depend on which countries hold the balance of economic power in the future and on demographic factors.

Notice how the example answer puts the information in different words than the original text. Here are some examples of paraphrase:

1. Original text: *globalisation - English No.1 language*
   Example answer: *With increasing globalisation, English has risen to global prominence. It is now ranked in top place amongst languages worldwide.*
2. Original text: *1.8 billion English speakers worldwide*
   Example answer: *Currently, 1.8 billion people speak English over the world.*
3. Original text: *English spoken over 5 continents (America, Asia, Australia, Europe, Africa)*
   Example answer: *Their (English speakers) countries of origin span the globe, taking in 5 continents from America to Asia and Australia.*

A. Now let's try to paraphrase the information for **Paragraph 2**. Complete sentences **1-6** using the correct form of the clue words in brackets ( ).

1. *English prerequisite for science:* (studies, science, write)
   In order to .... science, English is a prerequisite today as the majority of .... publications
   are .... in English.

2. *Knowing English allows access to knowledge on the Internet:* (wealthy, inform, know)
   The internet is a .... of .... but this is only accessible to those with a ....
   of English.

3. *Working internationally requires the ability to speak English:* (beneficial, attendee, hold)
   Speaking English may prove a tremendous .... for those .... international events
   .... in English.

4. *Globalisation now necessitates a knowledge of English for travelling purposes:* (survival, globe, normal)
   If one is to .... in this world of increasing ...., they need to speak English, since a basic
   proficiency in the language has now become the ....

5. *Knowledge of another language indicates ability and dedication:* (fluent, demonstration, commit)
   .... in a language other than your own .... not only intellect, but ...., too.

6. *English is integral to the entertainment industry:* (cultural, lyrical, annoyance)
   Every aspect of popular .... has been influenced by English from music .... to movies so
   learning English helps you not to be dependent on .... subtitles.

B. Now, using Question **A** above to help you, write a complete answer for **Paragraph 2**.

....

....

....

....

Tip: *A good way to make sure you paraphrase and use your own words is to try to choose different words from the original text when you are making your own notes in the first place. Then, use only your notes to write your answer and don't look at the original text again.*

C. When you made your notes for **Paragraph 3** in the first place, you probably wrote down **key words** from the original text just as in the example here:

Paragraph 3
- economic dominance - English-speaking countries being eroded
- Asian economies growing
- Asian countries now source: not recipient cultural/economic flows
- populations: rich countries ageing
- young with disposable income increasingly from Asia/Latin America than USA
- sea change - school curricula - Chinese second language, Australia

Instead, you could have written the notes in your own words. This makes the paraphrasing process easier. Rewrite the notes above using your own words. The first few notes have been done as an example.

Paragraph 3
- English speaking countries no longer have powerful economy
- Asian economies no longer weak
- Asian countries now dictate cultural and economic trends
  Other factors that could affect the future role of English:
  - ....
  - ....
  - ....

D. Now write a full answer for **Paragraph 3**, using your new notes. *If you need help, check the example notes.*

Exercise 5
The final paragraph should summarise the key points of your essay.

A. What is the key summary point of each paragraph (1-3) of your essay? Choose **A**, **B** or **C**.
   Paragraph 1
   A. In a relatively short time, English achieved world dominance.
   B. English has become a global language although its future as a No.1 language is uncertain.
   C. Many factors affect the prominence given to English as a global language.

   Paragraph 2
   A. There are very few areas today that English has not influenced in some way.
   B. It is often frustrating in the modern world if you do not know English.
   C. A knowledge of English improves your job prospects.

   Paragraph 3
   A. Languages other than English will become popular in the future.
   B. A change in the balance of global economic power could impact on English usage.
   C. The future will see many changes, both economic and demographic.

B. *First check your answers to Question **A**. Then try to write your complete final paragraph below.*

....

....

....

....

C. Compare your essay with the example essay below:

With increasing globalisation, English has risen to global prominence. It is now ranked in top place amongst languages world-wide. Currently, 1.8 billion people speak English over the world. Their countries of origin span the globe, taking in 5 continents from America to Asia and Australia. Not surprisingly, English is the most popular language to learn. There is a constant demand to learn the language which is the lingua franca today in a wide range of fields, from medicine to computing. How long English will remain secure in its position as the No.1 language will depend on which countries hold the balance of economic power in the future and on demographic factors.

Today, there are many examples of the need for English. Firstly, in order to study science, English is a prerequisite today as the majority of scientific publications are written in English. In addition, the internet is a wealth of information, but this is mostly accessible to those with a knowledge of English. Furthermore, speaking English may prove a tremendous benefit for those attending international events held in English. If one is to survive in this world of increasing globalisation, you need to speak English, since a basic proficiency in the language has now become the norm. Also, fluency in a language other than your own, demonstrates not only intellect, but commitment, too. English is also necessary as every aspect of popular culture has been influenced by English, from music lyrics to movies, so learning English helps you not to be dependent on translation.

In the future, English may decrease in importance as English speaking countries no longer have the powerful economy they once did. Asian economies that were previously weak are now dictating cultural and economic trends. In addition, the populations of rich English-speaking countries are ageing, which will result in a decline in English speakers. Furthermore, young people with disposable income are increasingly from Asian and Latin American countries rather than the USA, meaning that non-English speakers are increasingly likely to dictate global issues in the future. A sea change in school curricula, that has seen Australia teach Chinese as a second language, reflects this.

In conclusion, it can be seen that whilst English plays a prominent role and justly merits its position as No.1 global language, its future role is uncertain. Changing social and economic factors could make the language less relevant than languages spoken by Asian countries over the coming decades.

Exercise 6

Now you try. The question below relates to the texts about *Communication* on pages 14-16.

Use the information from the four texts you read in Task 2 (pages 14-16) to write an essay (200-230 words) for your science teacher describing the impact of the mobile phone in modern communication.

A. Follow these steps to answer the question.
1. Read the texts again **for gist** to remind you of what they are about. Make a short note of each text's topic.
2. Decide what information is important for your essay and choose a topic for each paragraph (**1-3**). **Paragraph 4** will be your summary/conclusion.
3. Make a note of which of the original texts have the information you need for each paragraph.
4. Find the key information you need from each original text and summarise it in your own words below.

Paragraph 1

....

....

Paragraph 2

....

....

Paragraph 3

....

....

B. Write your full essay answer. Remember, the final paragraph should summarise what you've said in the first three paragraphs. You may want to stop and make a few **summary notes** on your first three paragraphs before writing the final one.
Don't worry too much about the length of your essay for now (if it is longer than 230 words). We will look at word limits later.

Check your answer for spelling, punctuation and grammatical accuracy.

Argument Essay: The balanced argument approach

Now we will focus on <u>another form of essay</u>: The argument essay.

Argument essays may take *a **balanced*** viewpoint or the form of a ***one-sided*** argument. A ***balanced viewpoint*** considers both sides to an argument, but ends with the writer's opinion. A ***one-sided*** argument either supports or opposes the topic of the essay title. The writer will only discuss one viewpoint, which is their own, throughout the essay. In this unit we will prepare you for writing an argument essay with a ***balanced*** viewpoint.

Pre-reading

Write down as many ideas as you can think of for your answers to these questions. Then, if possible, discuss your notes with a partner.

1. Who buys designer goods?
2. Do you think designer goods are better than ordinary products?
3. Are designer goods popular in your country? Why?/Why not?
4. Do you think other people envy those with designer goods?
5. Would you ever buy counterfeit designer goods? Why?/Why not?
6. Does buying designer products take away work from local designers? Why?/Why not?

Exercise I

Read the texts about *Designer goods* and social and ethical concerns related to buying such products. Try to get a general understanding of what they are about. Write a note under each text about its general topic.

Text A

FROM COTTON TO CONSUMER

THE MAKING OF A DESIGNER TEE

COTTON   CUTTING   SEWING

DYEING   FINISHING   TRANSPORT

MARKUPS

TOTAL COST	$6.70
SOLD TO RETAILER	$15.00
SOLD TO YOU	$50.00

* All costs are estimates based on our own experience and information from vendors we've worked with.

Note: ....

Text B

John's Blog
Designer products

It's not about price, it's about competing with everyone around you, keeping up with the Joneses. And for what? To look the flashiest? To get that 'feel good' factor from wearing a big name? Readers, I have news for you: You are an adult and if you haven't figured this out yet, it doesn't matter what other people think of you, unless you are a Hollywood celebrity out to impress on the red carpet. No, the only time another person's opinion matters is at a job interview, because a job will provide you with an income to live an independent existence. Your potential boss is not looking at your wardrobe; he or she is looking at a single outfit. But even in that instance, guess what? Unless you have the Lacoste or YSL logo on your button down collared shirt, your boss will have NO IDEA how much you spent on your clothing. As long as you look presentable, that is what matters and it does not take a £300, a £200 or even a £100 shirt to do that. No product ever justifies the designer price tag.

Far better to buy great quality clothing from independent and possibly even local artists/artisans. You will get a unique 'designer' look but without the designer cost attached! So don't be swayed by the big names. Be sensible, buy into quality, not a designer brand! You will still look great at a fraction of the cost!

Note: ....

Text C

Merridale School Fashion Show: Reminder from Principal

This coming Friday our school will be staging a fashion show, featuring designs by our talented students. In response to a school project highlighting the social and ethical concerns of the designer industry, the students have created stunning designs out of low-cost fabric.

This show will prove that fashion doesn't need to cost a small fortune. Quite apart from the friction caused between students who sport designer clothes and those who don't, wearing designer goods is questionable for many reasons. We should support local talent - and that includes our students - not overpaid designers who profit at our expense!

So, please show your support for our students and promote local talent and come along to our show! You won't be disappointed!

Note: ....

Text D

Police alert: Circular letter to neighbourhood

We have been informed that a door-to-door salesman has been operating in the neighbourhood. He purports to sell designer clothes at knock-down prices. In reality, the clothes are cheap counterfeits and of extremely poor quality.

Purchasers should be aware that buying counterfeit goods is a criminal offence, as indeed is, of course, the manufacture and selling of such goods.

If you should be accosted by anyone selling fake designer clothing, please contact us immediately on the number below. Thank you in advance for your co-operation,
Surrey Police HQ, Worplesden. (04834 4792740)

Note: ....

Exercise 2
Look at this example question:

> *Designer goods: are they worth it?*
> *Use the information from the four texts you read (pages 32-33) to write an essay (200-230 words) for your teacher*
> *on some of the social and ethical issues involved in buying designer goods.*

The question above is an argument essay. Your plan will be influenced by your opinion. You must put forward a **balanced argument**. First you need to decide whether you think designer goods are worth it from an ethical and/or social viewpoint.

It might help first to *brainstorm* for ideas.

Here is an example of the brainstorming process:

Brainstorming
Before you plan your essay, spend a couple of minutes thinking of as many ideas as you can for what to say. This is known as *brainstorming*. After you brainstorm, pick your best ideas and then quickly organise them into paragraphs in a logical way.

Step 1
Using your own ideas and information from the preceding texts, write down as many ideas as you can think of
(*in your own language, or in English – it doesn't matter*). Spend about a minute doing this.

Designer goods

Advantages
- always consistent quality
- designer goods made from best materials
- guaranteed quality
- faulty goods easily replaced
- designer goods more unique than high street brands
- industry promotes more creativity
- owning designer products creates a feel-good factor

Disadvantages
- ridiculously over-priced
- many designer items produced in 'sweat shops' abroad
- difficult to tell 'fake' from real product
- designer products more 'showy' than practical
- some designer products as good as high street brands
- no benefit to local economy
- prestige symbol only for wealthy
- designer goods encourage theft
- those who can't afford designer goods feel inadequate
- peer competition (school/work) to possess designer goods
- growth of black market: fake designer goods

Step 2
Don't worry! Not all your ideas will be great or relevant to the topic. **Pick the best** ones and use them in your answer. If you have a lot of good ideas, then just pick some. Remember, you should only write about 200-230 words and you don't have much time. Choose a few key ideas and finish your plan.

Note
Which way do you think the writer will argue? **For** or **against** designer goods?
Hint: count disadvantages compared to advantages. Then, before continuing, decide which points refer to social and ethical issues. Underline the relevant points from the above task.

Your answer should be as set out below:

Social issues: ❖ prestige symbol only for wealthy   ❖ those who can't afford designer goods feel inadequate
                      ❖ peer competition (schools/work) to possess designer goods

Ethical issues: ❖ many designer items produced in 'sweat shops' abroad   ❖ no benefit to local economy
                      ❖ designer goods encourage theft   ❖ growth of black market: fake designer goods

Now, use your ideas from Step 2 to organise your ideas into paragraphs:

Your essay plan will be influenced by **your opinion**. You must put forward a balanced argument. If you disagree with the statement (as indicated by the content of the essay plan notes above), here is what you will write in each paragraph:

Paragraph 1: Introduce the topic in your own words and say what you are going to do.
Paragraph 2: Briefly look at the points supporting the argument that designer goods are good value.
Paragraph 3: Examine the **social issues** related to buying designer goods.
Paragraph 4: Examine the **ethical issues** surrounding the buying of designer goods.
Paragraph 5: A general summing up, voicing **your personal opinion** on the subject.

Note
The order in which social/ethical issues are dealt with is unimportant. i.e paragraphs 3 & 4 can be interchanged in position in the essay.

An example of an essay plan with content-related paragraphs is set out below:

Paragraph 1:   Who buys designer goods, why they are popular. Why buying designer goods raises social and ethical concerns.
Paragraph 2:   • prestige factor
                 • guaranteed quality
                 • unique product
Paragraph 3:   **Social factors**
                 • creates a social divide rich/poor
                 • those who can't afford them feel inadequate
Paragraph 4:   **Ethical factors**
                 • local economy not supported
                 • crime encouraged: counterfeiting and theft

Now let's look at the **finished essay** based on the notes. Read the essay and the tips carefully.

Sentence 3 introduces the essay topic. **Sentence 4** sets out what the writer is going to analyse.

Linking words, like the ones underlined, add emphasis and structure to the essay	Designer goods undoubtedly confer status and kudos on their owners. The term 'designer' additionally guarantees quality and uniqueness not seen in high street brands. <u>However</u>, do designer goods justify their hefty price tag and is buying into designer brands, justifiable from both a social and ethical viewpoint? <u>Here I will examine the pros and cons of buying designer goods.</u>
	<u>First and foremost</u>, designer goods are made from quality products and last longer than high street brands. The initial outlay on a designer product is therefore justified by its durability compared to cheaper non-designer items. <u>Additionally</u>, designer goods, being a limited range, are more unique than ordinary products. Buyers feel the ability to 'stand out from the crowd' which gives them a 'feel good' factor not achievable from buying ordinary, everyday items.
Notice how linking expressions are used in each paragraph to make the text flow and read well. You must link your ideas together.	<u>However</u>, detractors of designer goods argue that it is not worth buying designer products, from a social and ethical standpoint. Socially, designer goods create rivalry between the 'haves' and the 'have-nots' in society. Not being able to buy designer goods makes some feel inadequate.
	<u>More important</u>, however, are the ethical issues raised by buying designer goods. Buyers who opt for designer products are not supporting their local economy and creative talent. Another, more worrying, point to consider is the crime factor. Those sporting designer goods are more likely to be mugged or have items stolen than someone wearing more mundane products. <u>Furthermore</u>, the market for designer goods has led to a surge in counterfeit fake designer products. Crime is therefore an outcome of the huge demand for designer goods which most cannot afford.
Use a summing-up phrase to summarise what you've said.	In conclusion, it can be seen that whilst designer goods offer quality, their shortcomings from an ethical and social viewpoint, undermine their value. Personally, from this aspect, I believe the disadvantages of buying designer goods outweigh their advantages.

Linking Expressions
So far, we've looked at *planning, timing, structuring paragraphs* and *brainstorming*. Soon, we will look at another important feature of good answers: linking expressions. The ideas in your answers must be linked together in a logical way. This makes what you write easier to read and understand. Notice the important role linking expressions play in the example answer above.

Exercise 3

Using linking word/phrases in an essay.
Below is an extract from an essay on why celebrities favour designer clothes. Choose the appropriate linking word from the box below to complete the gaps.

Note: More than one option may be possible.

however	first and foremost	not to mention	therefore	so	moreover

Essay extract
There is nothing quite like being unique. **(1)** ...., it comes at a price, when you buy designer clothes. If you are a Hollywood celebrity, cost is irrelevant but if you are an ordinary person, designer clothes are normally a rare luxury. **(2)** .... why do we try to emulate celebrities when we don't have a celebrity pay packet **(3)** .... the fact that most of us have few occasions to wear designer clothes? Well, **(4)** .... designer clothes are definitely better quality than off-the-peg ones. **(5)** ...., designer clothes have more original designs than high street brands, **(6)** .... you can rest assured that someone else is highly unlikely to be wearing the same designer dress as you to a party!

Exercise 4

Now it's your turn to write an argument essay. Look at the essay topic below.

Use the information from the four texts you read (pages 32-33) to write an essay for you teacher (200-230 words) on whether or not it is right to spend money on designer clothes when there is so much world poverty. Give your opinion with reasons and arguments. You should plan your essay before you start writing. Think about what you want to say and make some notes to help you.

A. Let's use the Balanced Argument approach. Brainstorm ideas. Think of as many as you can to support both sides of the argument.

B. Now select your best ideas and organise them into paragraphs.

Paragraph 1 (Introduction)

Paragraph 2: ....
....

Paragraph 3: ....
....

Paragraph 4: ....
....

Paragraph 5 (Conclusion)

C. Now write your full answer. Give yourself 30 minutes. Then check your answer for mistakes at the end of that time.
Try and use as many linking words as possible to help your essay read better.

Focus:

Extended Writing Task 4

This section will help you prepare for Task 4 of the ISE III exam, Extended Writing.

Main objective:

To practise the nine possible kinds of Writing task in this section.

- descriptive essay
- discursive essay
- argument essay
- article (magazine or online)
- informal email
- informal letter
- formal email or letter
- review
- report

Topics:

The following topics are covered in the ISE III exam.

- Independence
- Ambitions
- Stereotypes
- Role models
- Competitiveness
- Young people's rights
- The media
- Advertising
- Lifestyles
- The arts
- The rights of the individual
- Economic issues
- Roles in the family
- Communication
- The school curriculum
- Youth behaviour
- Use of the internet
- Designer goods
- Equal opportunities
- Social issues
- The future of the planet
- Scientific developments
- Stress management

Timing and Word Count

As with Reading into writing Task 3, it is recommended that you spend 40 minutes on this task and you are also expected to write between 200-230 words. Remember to leave yourself five minutes at the end to check your answer for grammatical, spelling and punctuation mistakes. A good plan will make your use of time more efficient and effective.

Sample Answer 1 Formal Letter

Extended writing

> A new coal power station has been proposed for your area. Write a letter of complaint to your local council (200-230 words) outlining why the plan should not be approved.
>
> You should plan your letter **before** you start writing. Think about what you want to say and make some notes to help you.

Plan

In the question, you are encouraged to plan your answer. Spend about 5 minutes thinking of what you want to say. Brainstorm ideas and then organise them into short notes for what to write in each paragraph. Look at the example plan below:

Paragraph 1: say why you are writing – dismayed with proposal for plant
Paragraph 2: first point – coal is the past; renewable energy is future; need to protect environment; morally wrong
Paragraph 3: second point – factory location near homes; pollution and emissions could cause health problems
Paragraph 4: third point – financial reasons; tourism is big industry; coal plant would put tourists off
Paragraph 5: summarise – council must vote no in interest of town

Answer

Now look at the **model answer** and the **tips** for letter writing.

Always start your formal letter correctly.
Dear Mr/Mrs/Ms [Surname] if you know the person's name, or, *Dear Sir* or *Madam* if you don't.

Clearly say your **reason** for writing in paragraph 1.

Use *linking phrases* to **connect** your ideas better.

This is a formal piece of writing, so **don't** use **contractions**, e.g. *I would* - not *I'd*.

When you make a point, always use examples or explain/develop it.

End your letter *Yours faithfully* if you don't know the person's name or *Yours sincerely* if you do.

Use a different **paragraph** for each point and have 2 or 3 main-body paragraphs in total.

Rhetorical questions can sometimes be a good way to make a strong point.

Summarise your point in the final paragraph. Use a summing-up phrase.

Dear Sir or Madam,
I write regarding the proposal to build a new coal power plant on the disused industrial site on Fork Road put forward last week. I read about this proposal in the Newrath News with dismay *and* I would compel the council to reject the scheme in the strongest possible terms.

First and foremost, our town should be looking to the future, not the past. *Surely*, that future lies in clean energy; renewable sources, such as solar power. We have a social responsibility to protect the environment and play our small part in fighting global warming. Building a coal plant, *therefore*, is morally wrong.

Additionally, the proposed site of the factory is close to built-up residential areas. Plant emissions would, *therefore*, endanger local people. More pollutants in the air could potentially cause serious health issues, *such* as asthma and other lung conditions. Do I need to remind the council of the primary school located just half a mile from the site?

Finally, tourism brings more money than any other industry into Baleford. Think of the consequences for that sector if a dirty, ugly coal factory appears. *In other words*, the long-term financial cost of building such a plant would be huge.

For all of the reasons outlined above, I suggest there is only one decision you can make: please vote no to this proposal in the interests of our town.
Yours faithfully,
Amelia Ray

Your turn!

Write an answer for the following question. Remember to plan your letter first.

A new nuclear power station has been proposed for your area. Write a letter of complaint to your local council (200-230 words) outlining why the plan should not be approved.	You should plan your letter **before** you start writing. Think about what you want to say and make some notes to help you.

Sample Answer 2 Article

Extended writing

> You decide to write a piece for your school magazine on the voting age, arguing that it should be lowered. Write your article (200-230 words).
>
> You should plan your article **before** you start writing. Think about what you want to say and make some notes to help you.

Plan

Look at the example plan below:

Paragraph 1: say why writing – get the voting age reduced

Paragraph 2: first point – current age 18; but can drive bike 16, car 17; strange; if can drive, can vote

Paragraph 3: second point – benefits of lowering age: give young people a say; make us more interested/engaged; we have important views to share

Paragraph 4: sum up – reduce voting age to 16

Answer

Now look at the model answer and the tips for article writing.

> Articles always have a title. Give yours a suitable one related to the topic.

> Introduce the topic in paragraph 1.

> This is an informal piece of writing, so you **can use contractions**, e.g. *I'm* not *I am*.

> Use colourful language to make your article interesting. This will also help you show off your vocabulary.

> Know a variety of **stock phrases** for introducing your opinion.
> For example:
> - *In my view, …*
> - *To my mind, …*
> - *To my way of thinking, …*
> - *As far as I'm concerned, …*

> Asking questions can be a good way to introduce the topic or a new point.

> You can address the reader directly; this helps to engage them.
> The purpose of an article is to catch and keep the reader's attention.

> You can use a variety of types of punctuation for emphasis or colour in your informal writing, e.g. ellipsis (...), exclamation mark (!) and so on.

> As with any form of writing, make sure to summarise what you have said in the final paragraph. Use a **summing-up phrase** (and also use linking phrases throughout).

The right to vote

Are teens interested in politics these days? Well, I'm here to argue that we are and that it's about time the government allowed us to have a proper say in our country's affairs. Wouldn't you agree?

We all know the legal voting age is 18. This is the age the government has decided we become responsible adults. Huh? So, let me get this straight: we can drive a motorbike aged 16 and a car a year later, but we're not responsible adults for another year after that. Hmmm ... Seems a bit dangerous having loads of crazy, irresponsible young people driving around, right? But, of course, it's not because, as everyone knows, we're neither crazy nor irresponsible. And that's why I think the voting age should be lowered to 16.

Not only would this give us a greater say but it would also encourage us to get interested in politics. Everyone's always complaining today about how we just don't care anymore. Not true. Teens are passionate about a lot of issues, such as the environment and equality. Give us a chance – show us that our views actually mean something and allow us to get involved and make a difference and we'll prove you wrong. We'll engage with politics like never before.

It boils down to this: our views matter and we should be given a voice in politics. For me, the decision to reduce the voting age to 16 is a no brainer! Teen power!

Your turn!

Write an answer for the following question. Remember to plan your article first.

> You decide to write a piece for your school magazine on how to get young people more involved in politics. Write your article (200-230 words).
>
> You should plan your article **before** you start writing. Think about what you want to say and make some notes to help you.

Sample Answer 3 Report

Extended writing

> You did a survey of the people in your school year to find out who their role models are for a school project. Write a report of your findings (200-230 words).
>
> You should plan your report **before** you start writing. Think about what you want to say and make some notes to help you.

Plan

Look at the example plan below:

Paragraph 1: say purpose – to report findings of survey; Year 8 High Downs

Paragraph 2: findings – 55%: parent or close relative; 25%: celebrity (sportsperson or musician/singer);
        20%: professional; 2%: peer

Paragraph 3: family an important source of inspiration; celebrity too; but surprisingly, professionals too; suggests celebrity culture not as influential as people think

Answer

Now look at the model answer and the tips for report writing.

State the **purpose** of your report in the first paragraph and give any relevant background information.

This is a formal piece of writing, so don't use contractions, e.g. *report is* not *report's*.

Give each paragraph a heading. The first paragraph is always *Introduction* and the last is *Conclusion(s)*.

Know how to present figures.

For example:

The majority ...
A minority ...
Over half ...
Just under half ...
A quarter ...
One in three ...

Start your report as shown and always use a subject field stating what it is about.

Be familiar with the use of the passive tenses, e.g. *The survey was conducted ... The students were asked ...*

Have 1 or 2 main-body paragraphs discussing the findings of your report.

In the final paragraph, draw conclusions from the findings of your report and/or summarise them.

To: Ms Hugh
From: Lavender Kyle
Date: 07 May
Subject: Report on findings of survey of Year 8 students asking who their role models are

Introduction
The purpose of this report is to outline the findings of a survey of students which asked them to discuss their role models. The survey was conducted on the students of Year 8, at High Downs Secondary School.

Findings
A majority of 55% of students reported that they considered a parent or other relative their role model. Just under a quarter of students cited a celebrity as their role model. Among those students who chose a celebrity, the most common celebrity type was sports professional, followed by musician or singer. Approximately one in five students chose a well-known figure from a field or career discipline that interested them, such as a scientist or engineer. A small minority of around 2% of students claimed their role model was a peer – someone they knew of the same age as them.

Conclusions
Clearly, family continues to play a very important role in the lives of young people and many continue to look for inspiration for how they should live their lives from close relatives. On the other hand, a considerable minority of students seem to find their inspiration in the achievements of celebrities and professional sports people. Perhaps, most surprising of all is that nearly as many young people look to respected professionals for inspiration as well as celebrity figures. Overall, the findings of this report suggest that the influence of celebrity on young people is clearly not as great as many would believe.

Your turn!

Write an answer for the following question. Remember to plan your report first.

> You did a survey of the people in your year to find out who their heroes are for a school project. Write a report of your findings (200-230 words).
>
> You should plan your report **before** you start writing. Think about what you want to say and make some notes to help you.

Sample Answer 4 Review

Extended writing

> You write for your school magazine and your latest assignment is to review a new exhibition that has just launched at the local art museum. Write your review (200-230 words).
>
> You should plan your review **before** you start writing. Think about what you want to say and make some notes to help.

Plan

Use inspiration from real life to help you come up with ideas. This makes brainstorming a lot easier and gives you more to say. Think about things you've experienced or heard about that you can use in your writing.

Look at the example plan below:

Paragraph 1: say what it is – Living Art; brand-new; on for 8 weeks; idea of two street artists, Jenny and Julian Aston

Paragraph 2: describe – wide variety; original and feels full of energy; 3 sections; street statues – inventive and interesting costumes; circus performers and gymnasts; artists using spray paints and bottles

Paragraph 3: highlights – street artists; very talented; interact with them – ask questions and try techniques

Paragraph 4: recommend? Yes – for all family; best: free of charge

Answer

Now look at the model answer and the tips for review writing.

In paragraph 1, think of the **who, what, when, how long** and **where**. Give basic information about the thing being reviewed.

In paragraph 2, describe the thing you are reviewing in detail.

In Paragraph 3, talk about the good or bad points of the thing being reviewed.

In the conclusion, state your recommendation (Would you recommend it? Who for? How much does it cost? Is it good value for money?).

Always give your review a title. This can simply be the name of the thing you are reviewing.

This is an informal piece of writing, so you can use contractions, e.g. It's not It is.

Think about your target reader and the writing type.

Target reader: this is for your school magazine, so it needs to be colourful and interesting to keep the reader engaged.

Writing type: this is an informal review.

Living Art

Living Art is a brand-new exhibition running for the next eight weeks at the Hueston Gallery. It's the brainchild of local couple and professional street artists Jenny and Julian Aston. The Astons have brought together some of the world's greatest street performers under one roof for this colourful show.

The first thing that hits you as you enter the exhibition hall is the variety of performers and art on display. This is a highly original exhibition, full of energy and movement. It's divided into three separate sections, the first of which, called Golden Silence, features street statues in some of the most inventive and interesting costumes you'll ever see. The next section, Stretch, is a sort of mix of circus performing acts and gymnastics. The final section, Notes and Sketches, features artists using all kinds of materials from spray paints to plastic bottles to create incredible works of art.

The highlight of this show for me was watching the street artists draw and build amazing pieces. They are unbelievably talented and consequently make their art look effortlessly easy. What I liked most about this section was the chance to interact with the artists. You could ask them questions and even try their techniques.

I would thoroughly recommend a visit to the Heuston Gallery for this exhibition. It's a great feast of live entertainment suitable for all the family and, best of all, entry is absolutely free of charge. Simply unmissable ...

Your turn!

Write an answer for the following question. Remember to plan your letter first.

> You write for your school magazine and your latest assignment is to review a new show, event or festival happening in your area.
> Write your review (200-230 words).
>
> You should plan your review **before** you start writing. Think about what you want to say and make some notes to help you.

TRINITY

I ntegrated S kills in E nglish

ISE III - CEFR: C1

PRACTICE TESTS
1-6

Your full name: ....
(BLOCK CAPITALS)

Candidate number: ....

Centre: ....

Time allowed: 2 hours

Instructions to candidates
1. Write your name, candidate number and centre number on the front of this exam paper.
2. You must not open this exam paper until instructed to do so.
3. This exam paper has *four* tasks. Complete *all* tasks.
4. Use blue or black pen, not pencil.
5. Write your answers on the exam paper.
6. Do all rough work on the exam paper. Cross through any work you do not want marked.
7. You must not use a dictionary in this exam.
8. You must not use correction fluid on the exam paper.

Information for candidates
You are advised to spend about:
- 20 minutes on Task 1
- 20 minutes on Task 2
- 40 minutes on Task 3
- 40 minutes on Task 4

Task 1 – Long reading

You are going to read about gossiping as a useful tool of communication.
Read the text below and answer the 15 questions that follow.

Paragraph 1

Gossiping certainly has had a bad press. The term is sometimes used to specifically refer to the spreading of dirt and misinformation. Certain newspapers carry 'gossip columns' that relate scandals and personal information. Indeed, to be labelled a 'gossip' is certainly far from complimentary and suggests a meddlesome, if not somewhat vindictive, personality at work who is not to be trusted with personal confidences. Undoubtedly the instigator of catty, idle chatter that fuels so many office and school rumours would be deservedly maligned. Such malicious gossip is usually an individual's way of getting back at their enemies or advancing themselves and such behaviour is considered destructive to all parties concerned. In addition, stories of internet gossiping and bullying, tragically ending in the suicide of the victim of such gossip, are rife in the media. It is this type of gossip that has caused gossiping to be viewed so negatively.

Paragraph 2

Interestingly, the origin of the word 'gossip' originally bore no indication of the negative connotations that would later be attributed to the term. Deriving from the Old English for 'godsibb', meaning godparents, the term was used to describe close friends with social and religious obligations. It was only later in the 16th century that the word began to take on a more negative meaning, describing a woman who delighted in talking about others. The link between females and gossiping, in turn, originated from a time when women gave birth in front of a female-only gathering. At such occasions, social chatter would be part and parcel of the proceedings, resulting in the evolution of the word 'gossip' to mean idle, female talk.

Paragraph 3

Still today, gossips are looked down upon by society, even if the gossip in question is a close friend. This still holds true today, even if the gossip is a close friend. A study by Turner and colleagues showed that friends who passed on gossip in a laboratory experiment lost their own friends' respect and as a result perceived them as less trustworthy, afterwards. Furthermore, regardless of gossip type (positive versus negative) or relationship type (friend versus stranger) the gossipers were always rated as less trustworthy after sharing the gossip. In fact, so destructive is the action of gossiping perceived, that its effects have been likened to blackmail. Both gossip and blackmail involve the disclosure of a secret but with the latter, the individual has more control over the information as they have the option of silencing the blackmailer with a bribe. With gossip there is no such recourse; the gossip exposes the secret without warning.

Paragraph 4

However, recent studies would seem to suggest that gossiping is not all bad. In a recent study, undertaken by psychologists at the University of California, Berkeley, it was found that talking behind someone's back resulted in meaningful social benefits. In one experiment, a participant acted as an observer between two game players. During the game, one of the players cheated, accumulating a score disproportionate to their playing skills and ability. The observer, hooked up to heart rate monitors, was shown to exhibit an increased heart rate as the 'cheater' emerged as the triumphant 'winner'. However, when permitted the opportunity, most participants sent a 'gossip note' to the next player cautioning them not to trust the cheater - an action that simultaneously worked to lower the participants' heart rates. Additionally, such participants reported feeling happier afterwards than those participants not warning the other player.

Paragraph 5

The conclusions drawn from the study suggest that gossip can play an important role in maintaining social order, a purpose that may have had some evolutionary benefit. Willer suggests that as our human ancestors began to live in larger groups, it became increasingly impractical to monitor the behaviour of all group members. This apparently gave rise to the evolution of linguistic practices, in particular, gossip, as a means for sharing reputational information about the past behaviours of group members. Linguistic practices like gossip allowed group members to track one another's reputation as trustworthy interaction partners, even if they could not personally observe others' behaviour themselves. With reputational concerns foremost, group members were forced to keep selfish motives in check or risk ostracism.

Questions 1-5 (one mark per question)

The text on the previous page has 5 paragraphs (1-5). Choose the best title for each paragraph from A-F below and **write the letter (A-F) on the lines below**. There is one more title than you need.

1. Paragraph 1 ....

2. Paragraph 2 ....

3. Paragraph 3 ....

4. Paragraph 4 ....

5. Paragraph 5 ....

A	An unpleasant parallel
B	Doubtful advantages
C	A change in meaning
D	Gossipers feeling good
E	A common perception
F	Gossiping as a form of social control

Questions 6-10 (one mark per question)

Choose the 5 statements from A-H below that are TRUE according to the information given in the text on the previous page. **Write the letters of the TRUE statements on the lines below (in any order).**

6. ....

7. ....

8. ....

9. ....

10. ....

A	Gossiping benefits the gossiper, alone.
B	Self-promotion is often a reason for gossiping.
C	Gossiping is a modern phenomenon.
D	Alternative perceptions of gossiping are fairly recent.
E	An individual who gossips is esteemed by society.
F	Social control is established through gossiping.
G	Gossiping can be more devastating than blackmail.
H	Physiological and psychological benefits are conferred on gossips.

Questions 11-15 (one mark per question)

Complete sentences 11-15 with a word, phrase or number from the text (maximum 3 words). **Write the word, phrase or number on the lines below.**

11. Most people believe that gossips are .... by society.

12. The original meaning of 'gossip' was devoid of the .... it has today.

13. A gossip is perceived as less .... by others.

14. Surprisingly, there may be .... for the gossip.

15. It is likely that gossiping originated to uphold ....

Test 1

Task 2 – Multi-text reading

In this section there are 4 short texts for you to read and 15 questions for you to answer.

Questions 16-20 (one mark per question)

Read questions 16-20 first and then read texts A, B, C and D below the questions. As you read each text, decide which text each question refers to. Choose one letter A, B, C or D and write it on the lines below. You can use any letter more than once.

Which text would be most useful for someone who:

16. questions societal values?   ....

17. describes payment methods?   ....

18. discusses spending potential?   ....

19. shows changes in income over time?   ....

20. refers to practical issues?   ....

Text A

Unusual currencies

In the modern world, card transactions are invariably favoured over cash. Portable and lightweight, cards are deemed more convenient than bulky coinage.

However, if we consider coins a hindrance, we should spare a thought for past civilisations where payment in exchange for commodities was a far more complex affair. Historically, people have assigned monetary value to a diverse range of objects. Ancient currencies often came in many bizarre shapes, sizes and formats, ranging from the edible (salt, peppercorns) to the somewhat impractical (large immovable stones).

Undoubtedly amongst the heaviest and most difficult to carry currencies in the ancient world were 'Raj Stones'. These huge limestone rocks, weighing up to 8 tons, were legal tender in Micronesia from 500 AD. Their sheer enormity prevented physical exchange, their ownership being secured by local knowledge instead.

Some of the more practical currencies, being portable, tended to double up as bodily ornaments. Lucky Lobi Snake charms adorned the necks of ancient Ghanaians. Made from cast iron, the serpent-shaped amulets acted as a form of currency whilst supposedly warding off danger. Similarly, inhabitants of the Democratic Republic of the Congo wore their currency, the 'Katanga Cross' around their necks as a decorative ornament.

Another form of currency, that of squirrel furs, indisputably conferred good luck on Russian traders during the Middle Ages. As squirrel fur became the currency of choice in Russia, the squirrel population declined. As a result, Russia was inadvertently spared the scourge of the Black Plague since squirrels carried the dreaded disease.

One of the most bizarre currency forms was probably the potato masher, traded by Bafian cultures occupying the modern-day country of Cameroon. These were no mere culinary utensils but highly-prized items.

Text B

Blog

It seems that today's youngsters are rolling in money. A recent survey by The Children's Mutual has revealed that children are now deriving income from multiple sources. Whether as a reward for completion of homework or good performance at school, or as an accumulation of points on a reward chart for good behaviour, children are literally coining in the money. Parents are apparently more than happy to dole out generous amounts of money to their offspring in exchange for fulfilling set tasks. As a result, the Daily Mail has revealed that children today have a disposable income that would be the envy of many past generations of children. Children who received on average £1.18 a week in 1987 now get £6.84 - a rise of nearly 500 per cent.

So that the sizeable incomes of the young aren't squandered, the government is proposing to teach finance to schoolchildren as young as five years old. Probably a wise move, since one report estimates that personal expenditure of young people contributes around £5 billion annually to the economy.

Text C

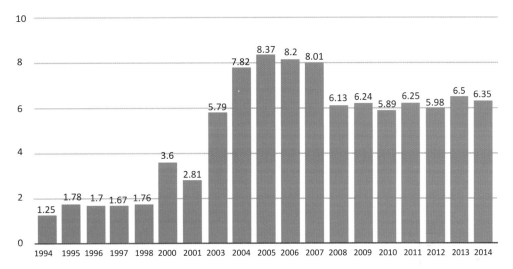

Pocket money weekly average in the United Kingdom between 1994 and 2014 (in GBP)

- Pocket money income from 1996-1998 averaged £1.71 weekly

- Pocket money showed the greatest fluctuation between 2000 and 2003

- The greatest increase (over 200%) in pocket money occurred between 2001 and 2003

- In 2005 pocket money was around 800% more than in 1994 (£1.25)

- Pocket money in 2014 was around 600% more than in 1994.

Text D

Celebrity incomes

Jasmine: Look at that! Says here that a top footballer earns around £100,000 a week! That's more than some top earners get annually!

Mark: Well they deserve it, don't they? Out in all weathers, playing football...

Lucy: Hardly a challenge, is it? They're paid to have fun kicking around a ball all day. Doctors and nurses are the ones who should receive huge pay packets. Not footballers and celebrities!

Dave: I agree. What would we do without the medical profession?

Mark: I know what you mean. But we need to be entertained, too.

Alison: Yes, but it's all about getting things in proportion, isn't it? Entertainers are important, but doctors and nurses are vital to society.

Tilly: Yes. That's why they should be paid more. Same goes for teachers, too. We all need education!

Ron: And don't forget refuse workers and cleaners. We couldn't do without them, either!

Questions 21-25 (one mark per question)

Choose five statements from A-H below that are TRUE according to the information given in the texts above.
Write the letters of the TRUE statements on the lines below (in any order).

21. ....

22. ....

23. ....

24. ....

25. ....

A	Early currencies had limited value
B	Often children's income is on a conditional basis
C	Earning potential is usually related to individual merit
D	Pocket money today is at an all-time high
E	Some ancient currencies had a dual function
F	Pocket money income remained fairly steady between 1996 and 1998
G	Today's youth have a lot of purchasing power
H	Modern currency is primarily practical

Questions 26-30 (one mark per question)

The summary notes below contain information from the texts above. **Find a word or phrase from texts A-D to complete the missing information in gaps 26-30**. Write your answers on the lines below.

Summary notes

Money

Currency

• Modern currency is designed to be **(26)**.. than in the past.

• The **(27)**.. of ancient currencies were anything but standard.

• Some ancient currencies had not just monetary value but were also **(28)**...................................... .

• The Bafian culture traded in a bizarre currency, namely a potato masher.

Income

• Children today are lucky to be rolling in money.

• **(29)**.. of income boost children's income today.

• In 2005, children's pocket money peaked at £8.37p weekly.

• Adult incomes are not always **(30)**.. to qualifications or skills.

Task 3 – Reading into writing

Use the information from the four texts you have read to write an article (200-230 words) for your school magazine. The topic of your article is 'Modern society and income'.

You should plan your article **before** you start writing. Think about what you want to say and make some notes to help you in this box:

Planning notes
(No marks are given for these planning notes)

Now write your article of 200-230 words. Try to use your own words as far as possible - don't just copy sentences from the reading texts.

When you have finished your article, spend 2-3 minutes reading through what you have written. Make sure you have answered the task completely. Remember to check how you made use of the reading texts, as well as the language and organisation of your writing.

Task 4 – Extended writing

You have been discussing the school curriculum in your class. You have been asked to write an essay (200-230 words) giving your opinion on the topic: "Nowadays changes need to be made regarding the school curriculum, so that it can meet the needs of society."

You should plan your essay **before** you start writing. Think about what you want to say and make some notes to help you in this box:

Planning notes
(No marks are given for these planning notes)

Now write your essay of 200-230 words.

When you have finished your essay, spend 2-3 minutes reading through what you have written. Make sure you have answered the task completely. Remember to check the language and organisation of your writing.

Test 2

Task 1 – Long reading

As part of your studies you are going to read about diet and how it has changed over the last half century.
Read the text below and answer the 15 questions that follow.

Paragraph 1

The decline in a nutrient-rich diet, exacerbated by an increasingly unhealthy lifestyle, is to blame for the recent and rapid rise in degenerative diseases amongst Westerners. In fact, our present day diet bears little relation to that of our predecessors, which was nutritionally rich due to personal, social and environmental factors. Most at risk are those born from the 60s onwards, who are most likely to exhibit the outcome of eating a poor diet, which increases the incidence of chronic disease patterns occurring later in life. It seems that the older we get, as a species, the less wise we are becoming, in eating habits, at least.

Paragraph 2

One major environmental factor that has drastically affected the quality of the Western diet is a change in farming methods. The favouring of monoculture* farming is in direct opposition to nature. Monocultures drain the soil of specific nutrients that would have been otherwise replaced by growing different crops. This has a knock-on effect, creating crops that are less nutritious, being deficient in vital minerals. As proof of this, recent government figures published show that fresh vegetables in the 1950s contained 50% more minerals than fresh produce half a century later. So we may think we are eating healthily by having our 'five a day' portions of fresh fruit and vegetables but what we are putting into our mouths, in fact, has little nutritional value.

Paragraph 3

The addition of certain minerals to the soil to stimulate uptake of micronutrients from the earth further depletes minerals in grown vegetables. One mineral particularly affected is selenium (Se) which, once removed from the soil, needs to be replaced. However, in the interests of crop yield and maximum productivity, this is not happening, leading to the appearance of chronic diseases in the population that are related to selenium deficiency. Replenishing the soil with the depleted minerals may prove costly in the short-term but in the long-term, it would reduce the medical costs of treating those with illnesses resulting from mineral-deficient diets.

Paragraph 4

We too are to blame, however, for our poor diet. It is all too easy to scapegoat modern farming methods as the cause of all our dietary woes when we should be paying more attention instead to what we eat. The huge popularity of fast food outlets bears testimony to our woeful eating habits. Children are especially liable to eat nutritionally poor diets. Over the last 50 years there has been a reduction in calorie intake (19% for boys and 29% for girls) whilst conversely, sugar consumption has increased dramatically. Fewer calories means a lower nutrient intake in the body resulting in lower immune strength and therefore increased susceptibility to disease.

Paragraph 5

Neither are schools blame-free for the nutritionally deficient diets of schoolchildren. School diets over the last half century show major deficiencies in all minerals and key vitamins. 86% of girls, for example, are getting below the recommended daily amount of iron, which is critical for good health. This is creating potential major problems for our young as they grow older in terms of chronic disease patterns related to a breaking down of the immune system; such a fear is supported by evidence that shows that childhood leukaemia is increasing in incidence. It is time, therefore, that schools made children more aware of the need to have a nutritious diet. Children should be given information, in the form of leaflets and talks, on what they should eat and what foods they ought to avoid. One example of foods that children should be warned off are processed foods. Poor diets of school children are being made even more nutritionally deficient by the increasing consumption of processed foods, like meat and cheese. A staggering 70-80% of the food we eat in the West is processed in some way, thereby reducing the mineral and vitamin content of food. In addition, children should be weaned off a high fat diet that in adulthood can lead to high levels of (blood) cholesterol and, in worst case scenarios, to high blood pressure, strokes and heart attacks. If the basics of healthy eating are instilled in children from an early age, then they are more likely to eat sensibly, as adults.

* Monoculture: the agricultural practice of producing or growing a single crop, or plant at a time.

Questions 1-5 (one mark per question)
The text on the previous page has 5 paragraphs (1-5). Choose the best title for each paragraph from A-F below and **write the letter (A-F) on the lines below**. There is one more title than you need.

1. Paragraph 1 ....

2. Paragraph 2 ....

3. Paragraph 3 ....

4. Paragraph 4 ....

5. Paragraph 5 ....

A	Diet affects health
B	A need for variety
C	Schools set good examples
D	Another poor agricultural practice
E	Better role models in the past
F	Time to take personal responsibility

Questions 6-10 (one mark per question)
Choose the 5 statements from A-H below that are TRUE according to the information given in the text on the previous page. **Write the letters of the TRUE statements on the lines below (in any order).**

6. ....

7. ....

8. ....

9. ....

10. ....

A	Children today consume fewer calories than in the past.
B	Food quality has improved greatly over recent years.
C	Only individuals are to blame, for having a poor diet.
D	Changing agricultural practices can be expensive.
E	Quality of crops has decreased as yield has increased.
F	Girls are at a very high risk from iron deficiency.
G	The effects of eating a poor diet only become evident in later life.
H	Poor agricultural practices can be implicated in illness.

Questions 11-15 (one mark per question)
Complete sentences 11-15 with a word, phrase or number from the text (maximum 3 words). **Write the word, phrase or number on the lines below.**

11. .... are a long-term result of a poor diet.

12. Changes in farming methods have led to the production of .... crops.

13. Children alone are not .... for their poor diets as schools feed them nutritionally poor meals.

14. Illness from consuming a poor diet arises when .... is compromised.

15. The vitamin and mineral content in food is also depleted as food ....

Task 2 – Multi-text reading

In this section there are 4 short texts for you to read and 15 questions for you to answer.

Questions 16-20 (one mark per question)

Read questions 16-20 first and then read texts A, B, C and D below the questions. As you read each text, decide which text each question refers to. Choose one letter A, B, C or D and write it on the lines below. You can use any letter more than once.

Which text:

16. sets out guidelines? ....

17. gives a descriptive account? ....

18. refers to the influential effect of Reality TV? ....

19. links the popularity of Reality TV to social factors? ....

20. discusses the psychological impact of Reality TV? ....

Text A

The Jerry Springer Show

The Jerry Springer Show is an American syndicated tabloid talk show hosted by Jerry Springer, a former politician. Since its inauguration in 1991, the show has run to a total of 3,891 episodes. Originally, it was very different from today's version of the show. Having started off as an issues-oriented and political talk show, the Jerry Springer Show is regarded now as pure entertainment of often dubious content. Highly controversial in nature, the show encourages conflict between studio guests and the audience.

The format has become highly stylised and has seen little variation over recent years. After a dramatic entrance, descending down a fireman's pole, centre stage, Springer introduces the first guest. Designed to be highly confrontational, the show airs grievances between the first guest and subsequent guests that appear later. Invariably, as accusations are aimed at other guests, the confrontation changes from the verbal to the physical. So seemingly staged are such physical confrontations that they are almost formulaic; the aggrieved guest is usually offered a glass of water to 'calm down'. This is then invariably thrown at the other guest who is perceived as having given offence. This then causes the level of aggression to escalate until nearly reaching a full scale punch-up. At this point the security officials interpose and try to resume order.

Despite its predictable format the Springer Show has proven so successful that for a while it was the top-rated daytime talk show in the US. Springer is less enamoured with his own show, however, and has stated: 'I would never watch my own show. I'm not interested in it. It's not aimed towards me. This is just a silly show.'

Text B

Reality TV

Simon: I think Reality TV programmes have great entertainment value! I love Big Brother. I've watched every series so far!

Jules: Yes, you never know what's going to happen on such shows - they're so unpredictable!

Annette: I think they're appalling. They humiliate the participants.

Lucy: Also they can have a negative impact on participants' self-esteem.

Mark: Come off it! Most people would kill to be on a reality show! Winners of Big Brother earn big money.

Belinda: Yes, also think of the fame and celebrity status you could enjoy!

Lorna: But such shows just create bad role models for society.

Jack: I agree. That's why society's in such a mess, today.

Text C

Application Information

Applications are being welcomed for the next episode of reality show 'Jungle Survival' which will be filmed on location in Australia this coming spring. Interested candidates should be over 18 years of age and physically fit, with high levels of stamina. Ability to cooperate as part of a team is essential, given the isolated and demanding location. All candidates should submit a written resume of skills, abilities and reasons for wanting to participate in the show.

Selected candidates will be invited to an initial screening interview. If passed, the successful candidates will then face an interviewing panel of six judges who will assess the candidates' suitability for the show. Following the successful completion of a psychological assessment and training exercise, candidates will be invited to take part in next season's show that will be aired on screens next autumn. Applicants should refer to the BBC website page to download a resume form. Completed forms need to be received by January 27th at the latest. There is a high level of interest for places on the show, so only successful candidates will be notified. If you pass the initial selection stage, you will be sent an e-mail or letter within a month of application. Previous candidates need not apply.

Text D

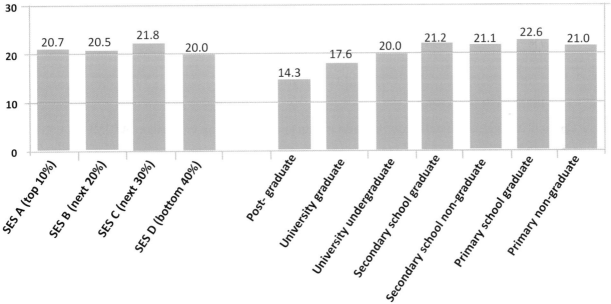

Percentage of People Watching Reality Television Frequently
(by Socio-economic Level and Education)

| SES = Socio-economic status | next 20% = those from 71% to 90% | bottom 40% = those from 1% to 40% |
| top 10% = those from 91% to 100% | next 30% = those from 41% to 70% | |

- Frequency of watching TV reality shows is not strongly correlated to socio-economic status.
- Regarding socio-economic status, reality TV shows are least popular amongst those in the lowest socio-economic bracket (bottom 40%).
- Regarding socio-economic status, reality TV shows are most popular with those in the second lowest socio-economic bracket (next 30%).
- Popularity of reality TV shows is more strongly correlated with education than socio-economic status.
- Reality TV shows are least popular amongst those who have completed the highest level of education e.g. post-graduate (14.3%).
- Reality TV shows are most popular amongst those who have one of the lowest levels of education e.g. primary school graduate (22.6%).

Questions 21-25 (one mark per question)

Choose five statements from A-H below that are TRUE according to the information given in the texts above. **Write the letters of the TRUE statements on the lines below (in any order).**

21. ....

22. ....

23. ....

24. ....

25. ....

A	The Jerry Springer show manipulates both the audience and participants.
B	Although disputes arise in the Springer show, rarely do they become physical.
C	Reality TV shows often fail to respect the participants.
D	Reality TV shows have no difficulty in finding participants.
E	Applicants for 'Jungle Survival' are initially selected on the basis of a resume.
F	Educational level better predicts a preference for reality TV shows than socio-economic status.
G	Fans of reality TV programmes are mostly people with a high level of education.
H	Socio-economic status clearly predicts a preference for reality TV.

Questions 26-30 (one mark per question)

The summary notes below contain information from the texts above. **Find a word or phrase from texts A-D to complete the missing information in gaps 26-30.** Write your answers on the lines below.

Summary notes

Reality TV shows

The impact on individuals and society:

- encouragement of aggressive behaviour in participants almost resulting in a **(26)**......................................
- not just verbal confrontations but also **(27)**..
- humiliation of participants, with an adverse effect on their psychology e.g. **(28)**...............................
- negative impact on society e.g. bad role models.

The appeal of Reality TV

- personal gain e.g. **(29)**...
- being unpredictable.
- financial incentives e.g. **(30)**..

Task 3 – Reading into writing

Use the information from the four texts you have read to write an article (200-230 words) for a local newspaper. The topic of your article is the appeal of Reality TV and why people both participate in such shows and watch them.

You should plan your article **before** you start writing. Think about what you want to say and make some notes to help you in this box:

Planning notes

(No marks are given for these planning notes)

Now write your article of 200-230 words. Try to use your own words as far as possible - don't just copy sentences from the reading texts.

When you have finished your article, spend 2-3 minutes reading through what you have written. Make sure you have answered the task completely. Remember to check how you made use of the reading texts, as well as the language and organisation of your writing.

Task 4 – Extended writing

You have been discussing the role of social media networks in society today, at school. You have been asked to write an email (200-230 words) to your teacher giving your opinion on whether social media networks cause more harm than good.

You should plan your formal email **before** you start writing. Think about what you want to say and make some notes to help you in this box:

Planning notes

(No marks are given for these planning notes)

Now write your email of 200-230 words.

When you have finished your email, spend 2-3 minutes reading through what you have written. Make sure you have answered the task completely. Remember to check the language and organisation of your writing.

Test 2

Test 3

Task 1 – Long reading

You are going to read about bullying and its long-term consequences. Read the text below and answer the 15 questions that follow.

Paragraph 1

Why would you want to send your child to a private school? The state schools in your area are pretty good. The teachers are qualified. The school seems to get plenty of students into good colleges and universities. There are plenty of extracurricular activities and sport facilities. Is it really worth the extra financial expenditure? Well, many parents believe it is for various reasons. It's a case of weighing up the pros and cons of both systems and deciding what is best, not only for your offspring, but for the entire family.

Paragraph 2

The main reason many parents begin to consider a private school is because the classes are considerably smaller than those of the state schools. Teacher to student ratios are typically 1:8 and class sizes are 10 - 15 students. Why are small class sizes and low teacher to student ratios important? Because they mean that your child will not get lost in the shuffle. Your child will get the personal attention that she or he needs and craves. Most state schools have classes numbering 25 students, or in some cases significantly more. Another point to consider is that most private schools are fairly small, usually 300 - 400 students. That's much smaller than a typical state school which will most likely have around 1000 students or more. It's very difficult to merge into the crowd or just be a number in a private school. If a student is struggling with a lesson, in a small class the teacher will realise this very quickly and will be able to address the learning issue on the spot rather than waiting weeks or months to fix it.

Paragraph 3

It would be incorrect and irresponsible to suggest that there are few outstanding teachers in state schools, but it is a fact that the majority of teachers in private schools have a first class degree in their subject and a high percentage, about 70 - 80 %, will also have a master's degree. When a private school Head of Department or Headteacher hires teachers, they look for competence in and passion for the subject a candidate will teach. They then review how the teacher actually teaches. They will look for charisma, an ability to instil discipline and an individual flair in their teaching style that will inspire their students. It is true to say however, that discipline is rarely an issue in private schools as students know that if they are disruptive they will be dealt with swiftly and without recourse. Finally they check out the three references (or sometimes more) from the candidate's previous employers to ensure that they are hiring the best candidate for the position.

Paragraph 4

Libraries, which are now called media centres, are now the focal point of some of the best private schools. Money has never been an object at these schools and similar older schools when it comes to books and research materials of every conceivable kind. But media or learning centres are the centre piece of almost every private school, small or large. Private schools also have first rate athletic facilities. Many schools offer horseback riding, hockey, rugby, tennis, football, gymnastics, diving and archery as well as a myriad of other sports. They also have the facilities to house and support these activities. Extracurricular activities are a major component of private school curriculums. Choirs, orchestras and drama groups are the norm in private schools and it is these extracurricular activities that are the first to be cut when a state school finds itself strapped for cash and needs to tighten its belt.

Paragraph 5

While the major focus at most private schools is preparing you for college, your personal maturation and development go hand in hand with that academic preparation. That way, hopefully you emerge from school with a good academic grounding and some great purpose for your life and understanding of who you are. In a private school it's cool to be smart whereas it is quite often the case in a state school that the more hardworking and academic students are frowned upon and seen as teacher's pets or geeks. This can lead to exclusion from the more popular student cliques. However, at a private school, rather than becoming an object of social ridicule, the smarter you are, the more respect you will get from your peers and the school will do its best to stretch your intellectual limits. That's one of the things private schools do exceptionally well.

Questions 1-5 (one mark per question)

The text on the previous page has 5 paragraphs (1-5). Choose the best title for each paragraph from A-F below and **write the letter (A-F) on the lines below**. There is one more title than you need.

1. Paragraph 1 ....

2. Paragraph 2 ....

3. Paragraph 3 ....

4. Paragraph 4 ....

5. Paragraph 5 ....

A	A broad educational experience
B	Sport rather than academic achievement
C	Quality rather than quantity
D	Developing character as well as intellect
E	Choosing the best school for your family needs
F	Strong leadership from the staff

Questions 6-10 (one mark per question)

Choose the 5 statements from A-H below that are TRUE according to the information given in the text on the previous page. **Write the letters of the TRUE statements on the lines below (in any order).**

6. ....

7. ....

8. ....

9. ....

10. ....

A	State schools have an acceptable success rate for university entrants.
B	Most children enjoy individual attention from their teachers.
C	Smaller schools tend to have less funding.
D	Private schools expect their staff to be high achievers academically.
E	A teacher's personality is more important than their qualifications.
F	An up-to-date research facility is of prime importance in a private school.
G	State schools have to prioritise where funds are used.
H	All schools find highly intelligent students a challenge.

Questions 11-15 (one mark per question)

Complete sentences 11-15 with a word, phrase or number from the text (maximum 3 words). **Write the word, phrase or number on the lines below.**

11. When choosing a school, parents need to consider the .... of both the state and private systems.

12. The .... of students to teachers are much lower in private schools.

13. A candidate for a teaching position must have at least .... from other jobs when they apply for a position.

14. When a school is short of money the non-academic activities are often .... to save money.

15. Private schools do their best to push a student's .... as far as they can.

Task 2 – Multi-text reading

In this section there are 4 short texts for you to read and 15 questions for you to answer.

Questions 16-20 (one mark per question)

Read questions 16-20 first and then read texts A, B, C and D below the questions. As you read each text, decide which text each question refers to. Choose one letter A, B, C or D and write it on the lines below. You can use any letter more than once.

Which text:

16. suggests a better way in which
public money could be used?   ....

17. hints at political action?   ....

18. refers to a comparison between reality and fiction?   ....

19. examines the pros and cons of space exploration?   ....

20. links space exploration to technological advances?   ....

Text A

Space Exploration

Tony: I think space travel opens up so many possibilities for mankind.

Jackie: It would be amazing to discover other life forms! It would be wonderful if aliens existed!

Dave: Waste of money if you ask me. That money could be spent on better things, like education.

Lorna: Yes, the money spent on space exploration could also be used to aid developing countries.

Tanya: I don't think we know enough about our own planet yet.

Annabel: And we are destroying it too! Imagine if we colonised other planets what would happen!

Simon: I think we may need to form space colonies on other planets soon if we continue to destroy our Earth!

Text B

Dear Editor,

I felt that I really had to write to voice my objection over the billions of dollars spent on space exploration annually. I was astounded to learn the other day, in a recent article published in your paper, that the cost of the Space Shuttle programme alone amounts to $1.5 billion per flight, the total cost of NASA's US Space Shuttle programme amounting to a staggering $200 billion!

Our health service is in dire need of funds, as is our educational system. Why is so much money being wasted on space travel that is of relevance only to NASA and those working on space programmes? Surely space exploration is a luxury, whilst health and education are necessities. I only hope that people like myself will be able to stir up opposition to the space programmes and make the government see sense before our country runs out of money for public funding. It's not right that people are being sidelined just to satisfy the curiosity of scientists! I want the money I pay on tax to be spent on more worthwhile projects.

Yours faithfully,
Vera Browning

Text C

Space exploration and the money spent on it can be an emotive subject. Indeed the billions spent on isolated projects do make the vast majority of people question the morality of such expenditure when there is so much suffering and poverty in the world. However, many overlook, or, are not aware of, the many benefits that space exploration has brought to mankind. It is these benefits that should be borne in mind when weighing up the pros and cons of spending money on space exploration.

For a start, water purification techniques that were developed for space exploration are being used in Third World countries, ultimately preventing disease and saving lives so it is not just the developed world that is benefiting from space exploration. In addition, we are seeing greater yields of crops thanks to space-driven technology, not to mention advances in medicine, from treatments for brain cancer to the development of more accurate thermometers. And these are just to name but a few of the space-driven technologies that are currently benefiting mankind.

The environmental benefits, too, are wide-ranging, as satellites in orbit provide valuable data about how our atmosphere is evolving. Data from studies of other planetary atmospheres in the solar system help us to understand ours. In fact, a countless number of space-motivated technologies have changed the face of society. It would be folly to put a stop to space exploration now when we are beginning to discover so much that will ultimately benefit all of humanity. Doing so would be tantamount to being a space age Luddite, trying to stop progress just so that we can keep an unsatisfactory status quo. Only the most foolish would adopt such a policy; and at what cost to mankind and its future survival?

Text D

Cost of recent Mars orbiter missions

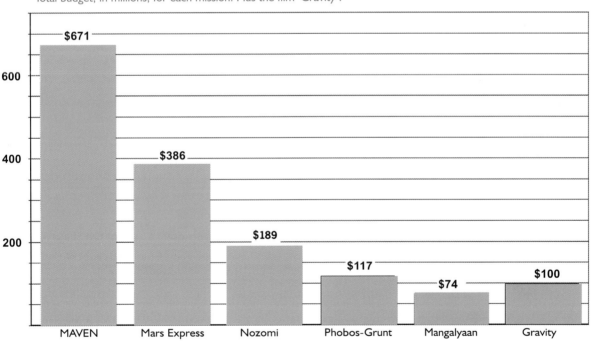

Total budget, in millions, for each mission. Plus the film 'Gravity'.

Relative cost of recent Indian Mars missions compared to US expenditure for film 'Gravity'.

- Maven mission was spawned by NASA's Mars Scout Programme. Mars Scout missions target a cost of less than $485 million, not including launch services, which cost approximately $187 million. The total project costs up to $671 million.
- Mars Express, Europe's first planetary mission cost almost 300 million US dollars. This includes the launch, the spacecraft, the scientific payload (including the lander) and operations.
- The cost of the Mars Express mission was over three times the cost of the Phobos-Grunt mission.
- 'Gravity' cost nearly a seventh of the amount spent on the most expensive mission ($671 million).
- The total cost of all the Mars missions totalled $1,437 million.

Questions 21-25 (one mark per question)
Choose five statements from A-H below that are TRUE according to the information given in the texts above.
Write the letters of the TRUE statements on the lines below (in any order).

21. ....

22. ....

23. ....

24. ....

25. ....

A	Money spent on space exploration is a controversial issue.
B	Only a limited few benefit from technologies developed from space exploration.
C	Space exploration is of no relevance to our planet.
D	The technologies developed from space exploration benefit not just medicine.
E	The full potential of space-related technologies is yet unknown.
F	Both the developed world and Third World countries are benefiting from space exploration.
G	Many would prefer money to be spent on human issues rather than space exploration.
H	In the US many jobs have been lost due to money spent on space exploration.

Questions 26-30 (one mark per question)
The summary notes below contain information from the texts above. **Find a word or phrase from texts A-D to complete the missing information in gaps 26-30**. Write your answers on the lines below.

Summary notes

Space exploration

Disadvantages and advantages

*   Alternative lifestyle possibilities are enabled by space exploration e.g. **(26)**... .

*   Space exploration could permit exciting discoveries e.g. other life forms.

*   Some believe other problems e.g. **(27)**....................................... should be prioritised.

*   Space-driven technology has benefited many fields e.g. medicine.

Expenditure related to space exploration

*   Money spent on space exploration exceeds that spent on other areas e.g. **(28)**.. .

*   Isolated NASA space projects, e.g. **(29)**.., exceed a billion dollars.

*   India's space missions, called **(30)**..., cost billions of dollars.

*   Hollywood films can be costly too, e.g. 'Gravity' cost more than India's Mangalyaan mission.

Task 3 – Reading into writing

Use the information from the four texts you have read, to write an article (200-230 words) for a science magazine. The topic of your article is whether money spent on space exploration is excessive and wrong.

You should plan your article **before** you start writing. Think about what you want to say and make some notes to help you in this box.

Planning notes

(No marks are given for these planning notes)

Now write your article of 200-230 words. Try to use your own words as far as possible - don't just copy sentences from the reading texts.

When you have finished your article, spend 2-3 minutes reading through what you have written. Make sure you have answered the task completely. Remember to check how you made use of the reading texts, as well as the language and organisation of your writing.

Task 4 – Extended writing

You have recently read an article in a newspaper titled: "Since more people are travelling abroad nowadays, it is necessary for individuals to have a greater awareness of other cultures." Write a letter (200-230 words) to the newspaper in order to give your opinion on the topic.

You should plan your letter **before** you start writing. Think about what you want to say and make some notes to help you in this box:

Planning notes

(No marks are given for these planning notes)

Now write your letter of 200-230 words.

When you have finished your letter, spend 2-3 minutes reading through what you have written. Make sure you have answered the task completely. Remember to check the language and organisation of your writing.

Test 4

Task 1 – Long reading

You are going to read about planet Mars. Read the text below and answer the 15 questions that follow.

Paragraph 1

Participants for a one-way trip to Mars were not in short supply, when NASA recently went out to recruit willing participants for permanent exile in space. The initial one hundred candidates selected range from an archaeologist to a singer and a 19-year-old student. Despite the fact that the candidates come from many different walks of life and boast a wide variety of talents and skills, all share unbounded enthusiasm in common, at the prospect of being marooned forever on the Red Planet. The majority of us, though, would probably have considerable reservations in voluntarily committing ourselves to such a project, as space is a dangerous place for fragile humans. Those willing to venture into space must negotiate health hazards, such as extreme temperatures, cramped quarters, long periods of isolation and the debilitating physiological effects of life without gravity. Now, recent research would seem to suggest that those who have reservations about travelling to Mars are somewhat justified.

Paragraph 2

Amongst the myriad of hazards associated with deep-space travel is prolonged exposure to unrelenting cosmic radiation. Such exposure is detrimental to DNA and can radically change its structure, thereby increasing the risk of diseases, such as cancer, developing. However, that is not the most worrying problem to contend with. Recent research with mice suggests that the first people to attempt a Mars mission will experience a further problem: brain damage. This would seem to be a real deal-breaker when it comes to sending astronauts to Mars, for how can astronauts operate highly sophisticated equipment and perform complex maintenance tasks if they suffer cognitive impairment to any degree? It seems foolhardy at least to put astronauts at such physical risk.

Paragraph 3

The research also suggests that cognitive and memory impairments caused by cosmic rays bombarding the brain in outer space may manifest themselves in just a few months. Previous studies had indicated that radiation exposure could cause cognitive impairment leading to the onset of Alzheimer's-like dementia later in life. The effect of cosmic radiation was believed to have a devastating effect on biological tissue over a lifetime. Now, recent research has turned up the worrying possibility that such trauma to the brain may manifest itself much earlier. According to Charles Limoli, Professor of Oncology at the University of California Irvine School of Medicine, such neural abnormalities could manifest themselves within two to three years.

Paragraph 4

Limoli's research was based on the study of mice subjected to doses of energetic charged particles similar to those found in galactic cosmic radiation. The mice used in the sample were aged at six months - the approximate age of astronauts in mouse years. As a result of exposure to the 'mind numbing' effects of radiation, free radical reactions in cells, known to instigate cancer, occurred within milliseconds. The physical effects of such reactions then became evident within weeks, as the irradiated mice were significantly impaired in their ability to explore new objects placed in their environment, a task that draws upon a healthy learning and memory system. "The animals that were exposed lost curiosity. They lost their tendency to explore novelty." says Limoli. The damage seen in the mice affected was akin to the defects seen in human brains suffering from neurodegenerative conditions which occur over the course of ageing. More worryingly still, the effects were irreversible.

Paragraph 5

Whilst the findings of Limoli's research raise serious questions about prolonged space travel, some scientists believe the issue not to be so cut and dry. Nathan Schwadron, Associate Professor of Space Plasma Physics at the University of New Hampshire, believes that while such findings are cause for concern, they might not be quite as disturbing as they might first appear. "I think that there is a potential risk here," states Schwadron, "but we really just don't understand it yet." Nevertheless, scientists are pressing ahead with advanced shielding technologies that could better protect astronauts on long-term missions into deep space. In addition, Limoli and his team are investigating pharmacological interventions that could protect brain tissue from cosmic radiation. The space scientists are not to be put off, apparently, by the results of one research study, however alarming the results may seem to be. After all, experiments on animals do not always accurately reflect how human physiology bears up under similar experimental situations. What may prove damaging for more vulnerable animal neural systems, may not prove so damaging for Man.

Questions 1-5 (one mark per question)

The text on the previous page has 5 paragraphs (1-5). Choose the best title for each paragraph from A-F below and **write the letter (A-F) on the lines below**. There is one more title than you need.

1. Paragraph 1 ....

2. Paragraph 2 ....

3. Paragraph 3 ....

4. Paragraph 4 ....

5. Paragraph 5 ....

A   Visible signs of neural damage

B   Not for everyone

C   Time frame for neural damage questioned

D   A more positive outlook

E   A decreased interest in space travel

F   Extensive effects on health

Questions 6-10 (one mark per question)

Choose the 5 statements from A-H below that are TRUE according to the information given in the text on the previous page. **Write the letters of the TRUE statements on the lines below (in any order).**

6. ....

7. ....

8. ....

9. ....

10. ....

A   The nature of people who are willing to travel to space is quite diverse.

B   Cosmic radiation has no visible effects.

C   Even short-term exposure to cosmic radiation is dangerous.

D   The effects of cosmic radiation may not be immediately apparent.

E   Scientists are less optimistic now about prolonged space travel.

F   Scientists are trying to counter cosmic radiation in a number of ways.

G   Cosmic radiation causes temporary damage to cells.

H   Mice exposed to cosmic radiation behave similarly to aged humans.

Questions 11-15 (one mark per question)

Complete sentences 11-15 with a word, phrase or number from the text (maximum 3 words). **Write the word, phrase or number on the lines below.**

11. It is to be expected that most people have .... about space travel.

12. Space travel is dangerous because it involves a ....

13. Cosmic radiation may affect the ability of astronauts to carry out ....

14. Effects of cosmic radiation may manifest themselves .... of exposure to the source.

15. Scientists believe that the findings of studies on cosmic radiation are not .... some might think.

Task 2 – Multi-text reading

In this section there are 4 short texts for you to read and 15 questions for you to answer.

Questions 16-20 (one mark per question)
Read questions 16-20 first and then read texts A, B, C and D below the questions. As you read each text, decide which text each question refers to. Choose one letter A, B, C or D and write it on the lines below. You can use any letter more than once.

Which text:

16. discusses the practical applications of learning? ....

17. analyses people's regrets? ....

18. offers a historical perspective? ....

19. mentions learning skills outside school? ....

20. describes a long-term policy? ....

Text A

The mid- to late- 1960s are known as a time when people were questioning the status quo and setting out alternative visions of how things should be done, in a wide range of fields, and education was one of the most important. Various "alternative schools" came into being, one of the most famous being Summerhill School. In fact, the origins of Summerhill go back as far as 1921, when it was founded in Germany by the teacher A.S. Neill. It later moved to Austria, then the U.K., but by the early 1960s its fortunes were fading as pupil numbers dwindled. Neill wrote a book about the school and his ideas, which became a best-seller, and interest in the school and his ideas revived.

The media labelled Summerhill as a "freedom school" or, less complimentary, "the do-as-you-please school". Neill himself was often portrayed as a hopeless idealist who encouraged anarchy in the classroom and the world outside, but he never wavered in his core belief that children are "innately wise and realistic" and have a right to freedom and happiness.

Neill was convinced that "normal" schools produced only citizens who were "docile, uncreative children who will fit into a civilisation whose standard of success is money." In contrast, Summerhill graduates left the school with a sense of self-worth and a range of what business people now value as "soft skills", like communication, empathy and teamwork.

Text B

Web forum

Tony: I remember when I was at school I had to learn stuff like algebra and geometry. After a while I just switched off and I never managed to grasp the idea. But I can honestly say I've never had to use any of it in my life.

Bill: But how do you know that for sure? Maybe if you'd understood it, you'd find it's useful after all. Have you never had to work out how much wallpaper you need to cover the walls in a room, for example?

Tony: No, I just pay a professional to do things like that. They do a much better job than I could, and anyway I've got more interesting things to do with my time.

Tina: All I can say is you're lucky to be able to afford it. I know home maintenance and DIY isn't everyone's favourite activity but it can really save a lot of money. More generally, though, as a lot of people say, there are plenty of things we learn at school that we don't realise are relevant until later in life?

Text C

Unsurprisingly, most schools claim to prepare students for the world of work, but the ethos at Stevendon High School goes far beyond mere words: the school's commitment to the principle pervades all aspects of school life.

Before they even join the school, prospective pupils attend an informal interview at their primary school to discuss their hopes and preferences for the future. The emphasis on employment continues during the first two years at Stevendon, then in the third year all pupils spend a day doing work experience at a local company. Two years later, this becomes a whole week spent with a different company, usually arranged by the students themselves.

Throughout their time at the school, students are provided with professional careers advice, which doesn't come cheap. In fact, it costs the school over £30,000 a year. Head Teacher Muriel Greenwood believes it's money well spent. "Schools often think they're fulfilling their commitments by offering final year pupils a lesson every week, taught by existing staff", she says, "but this is too little, too late. Teachers aren't trained to be careers advisors, so we bring in professional help. It's part of a co-ordinated programme that aims to make students aware of the employment options available, and how to make the most of them."

Text D

Things we wish they'd taught us at school

Almost half of adults in a recent poll said they felt that what they learnt at school hadn't prepared them for real life. Here are eight of the most common life skills people wish they'd been taught:

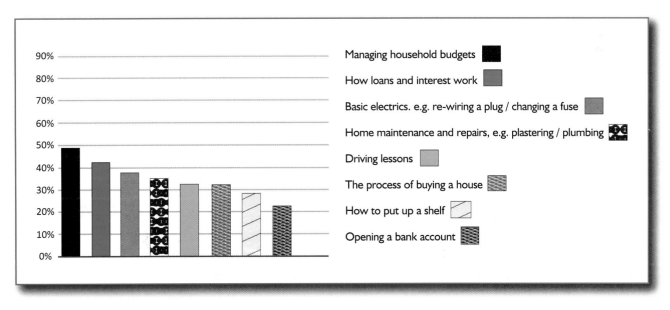

Questions 21-25 (one mark per question)
Choose five statements from A-H below that are TRUE according to the information given in the texts above.
Write the letters of the TRUE statements on the lines below (in any order).

21. ....

22. ....

23. ....

24. ....

25. ....

A People now realise that A.S. Neill's ideas were ahead of their time.

B Press reaction to A.S. Neill and his school was often hostile.

C One aim of Summerhill is to help its students be useful to society.

D Tony found maths classes boring and difficult.

E It's quite often said that the usefulness of school subjects isn't immediately apparent.

F Muriel Greenwood thinks Stevendon serves its pupils better than other schools.

G The survey was conducted using a random sample of students.

H Half of the skills people regret not learning are in the area of finance.

Questions 26-30 (one mark per question)
The summary notes below contain information from the texts above. **Find a word or phrase from texts A-D to complete the missing information in gaps 26-30**. Write your answers on the lines below.

Summary notes

- 1960s a time when people presented (26).. e.g. A.S. Neill / Summerhill in education

- Belief that standard education was not about making pupils fit in with society

- Feeling that some school subjects are not (27)... to real life (although this may not become clear until later)

- Some schools prepare students for employment via practical (28).. programmes (to help learn workplace skills)

- Important to let students see what (29).. are open to them

- Many believe school failed to teach them several useful (30)...

Task 3 – Reading into writing

Use the information from the four texts you have read to write an essay (200-230 words) for your teacher with the following title: **Education for Life?**

You should plan your essay **before** you start writing. Think about what you want to say and make some notes to help you in this box:

Planning notes

(No marks are given for these planning notes)

Now write your essay of 200-230 words on the lines below. Try to use your own words as far as possible - don't just copy sentences from the reading texts.

When you have finished your essay, spend 2-3 minutes reading through what you have written. Make sure you have answered the task completely. Remember to check how you made use of the reading texts, as well as the language and organisation of your writing.

Task 4 – Extended writing

You have been discussing the decline in good quality TV today, in your Media Studies class. You have been asked to write a formal letter (200-230 words) to the owner of a well known TV channel, to complain about the steady decline in the quality of their TV programmes over the last decade. Give examples to support your points.

You should plan your letter **before** you start writing. Think about what you want to say and make some notes to help you in this box:

Planning notes

(No marks are given for these planning notes)

Now write your letter of 200-230 words.

When you have finished your letter, spend 2-3 minutes reading through what you have written. Make sure you have answered the task completely. Remember to check the language and organisation of your writing.

Test 5

Task 1 – Long reading

You are going to read about non-verbal communication. Read the text below and answer the 15 questions that follow.

Paragraph 1

Ever had an uneasy feeling when someone was telling you something that didn't ring true, even when you had no grounds for suspicion that the communicant wasn't telling the truth? Or maybe someone's facial expressions didn't quite synch with their emotional expressions? If so, you were probably picking up on unintentional, subconscious messages being conveyed by the speaker, indicating their real thoughts, in conflict with what they were overtly communicating to you. Such messages are *implicit* and conveyed in body language, as distinct from *explicit* messages which are the basis of everyday verbal communication. It is these implicit messages that can leave us with a vague feeling of unease or distrust of the speaker concerned. We know that something is wrong but we just can't put a finger on it.

Paragraph 2

Nowadays we can better understand the hidden code behind body language. Social psychologist, Desmond Morris, is to be credited with bringing non-verbal communication into the public eye. Author of 'The Naked Ape' (1967) and 'Body Watching' (1985), Morris, in his groundbreaking books, drew parallels between animal and human body language to unravel the hidden meaning behind our forms of non-verbal communication employed in everyday life. Such forms of non-verbal communication include facial expressions, the tone and pitch of the voice, gestures displayed through body language (kinesics) and the physical distances between the communicators (proxemics). Tellingly, these non-verbal signals can give clues, additional information and meaning over and above spoken or verbal communication.

Paragraph 3

Such non-verbal cues can relay a wealth of information to the listener, although often at a subconscious level. Non-verbal messages can convey the speaker's real feelings, thereby providing negative or positive feedback to the other person, distancing or reinforcing a relationship. Classic examples of acceptance and encouragement are a held gaze, closeness of body position and relaxed posture. Contrastingly, a speaker who has their arms or legs crossed, with their body turned away from the listener, signals a hostile, defensive attitude to the latter, which may be further emphasised by increased personal distance between themselves and the listener. 'Mirroring' is another way that we can ascertain our relationship to the speaker. Matching of the listener's posture, in facial expressions or gestures, indicates liking and acceptance.

Paragraph 4

Nowhere is body language more important than in our work and personal relationships. Whether we are sizing up a potential partner or attending a job interview, it is often what we communicate non-verbally that will make or break a situation. The expression 'it's not what you say, it's what you do' is never more true than during job interviews. Your body language can have a significant impact on how you are perceived and so you have to be aware of it from the moment you step into the interview room. You are being judged before you've uttered your first word. The average time it takes for an interviewer to decide whether a candidate will be accepted for a job is within a time frame of 3 minutes - often even less. It therefore makes sense to be acquainted with the working basics of body language that can otherwise prove such a potential minefield in job interviews. With the plethora of sites on the internet and in magazines, offering helpful tips on improving body language for personal gain, it is fairly easy today for the layman to get a grasp of the ins and outs of non-verbal communication.

Paragraph 5

A word of warning, however, to the uninitiated: the interpretation of body language is not infallible, since several factors may obfuscate non-verbal messages and how they are interpreted. One factor is conscious manipulation of body language by the speaker. The same self-help books that teach people to interpret body language, also convey the information, unwittingly or otherwise, as to how to 'fake' non-verbal signals, such as gestures and eye contact. An individual can easily learn to simulate interest in a person or job and to hide their real feelings, for example. Other factors that complicate the interpretation of non-verbal communication are cross-cultural differences. Whilst in some countries, such as Japan, prolonged eye contact can be seen as disrespect, in Western cultures it signifies interest. Additionally, personal spacing in British culture is significantly greater than in Middle-Eastern cultures, leading to confusion and often discomfort if such differences are not understood.

Questions 1-5 (one mark per question)

The text on the previous page has 5 paragraphs (1-5). Choose the best title for each paragraph from A-F below and **write the letter (A-F) on the lines below**. There is one more title than you need.

1. Paragraph 1 ....

2. Paragraph 2 ....

3. Paragraph 3 ....

4. Paragraph 4 ....

5. Paragraph 5 ....

A Open to misinterpretation
B Information through non-verbal communication
C What constitutes non-verbal language
D Conflicting messages
E Cultural disadvantages
F Why body language is important

Questions 6-10 (one mark per question)

Choose the 5 statements from A-H below that are TRUE according to the information given in the text on the previous page. **Write the letters of the TRUE statements on the lines below (in any order).**

6. ....

7. ....

8. ....

9. ....

10. ....

A Body language can communicate more than verbal communication.
B Non-verbal language can be consciously altered.
C Interpreting body language requires special expertise.
D Awareness of body language and its relevance is very recent.
E Often body language can only be understood at a subconscious level.
F Non-verbal communication is assessed in potential employees.
G Body language does not convey a universal meaning, always.
H Faking body language is extremely difficult.

Questions 11-15 (one mark per question)

Complete sentences 11-15 with a word, phrase or number from the text (maximum 3 words). **Write the word, phrase or number on the lines below.**

11. Often when a speaker's words are .... their body language, we feel they are untrustworthy.

12. A speaker may be .... one emotion, but their body language might tell a different story.

13. Body language conveys .... to what is actually being said.

14. Non-verbal communication can have the effect of .... the relationship one might have with other people.

15. Unfortunately, the interpretation of body language ...., leading to misunderstandings.

Task 2 – Multi-text reading

In this section there are 4 short texts for you to read and 15 questions for you to answer.

Questions 16-20 (one mark per question)

Read questions 16-20 first and then read texts A, B, C and D below the questions. As you read each text, decide which text each question refers to. Choose one letter A, B, C or D and write it on the lines below. You can use any letter more than once.

Which text:

16. informs about normal sleeping patterns?   ....

17. identifies sleeping disorder types?   ....

18. offers solutions for a specific sleeping disorder?   ....

19. illustrates how adults can differ vastly in sleeping patterns?   ....

20. suggests that lack of sleep may not be a disadvantage?   ....

Text A

Sleep disorders

It is a common misconception that insomnia is the only sleep disorder and that sleeping problems are just one form or another of this problem. In total, there are more than 100 different sleeping and waking (since the latter is directly connected to the former) disorders. They can be grouped into four main categories: problems falling and staying asleep (insomnia), problems staying awake (excessive daytime sleepiness), problems sticking to a regular sleep schedule (sleep rhythm problem) and unusual behaviours, such as sleep-walking during sleep (sleep-disruptive behaviours). All types of disorder are equally debilitating in their own way and lead to at least a temporary loss of normal functioning which can have a knock-on effect in everyday life whether at home or at work. Loss of concentration and forgetfulness are just some of the short-term symptoms of disturbed sleep.

In some cases, sleep disruption, such as insomnia, may be acute and not require medical attention. However, when any of the conditions become chronic, it is time to seek medical attention, since some disorders, such as excessive daytime sleepiness, may reveal an underlying physiological problem, such as a low thyroid function. Other disorders, such as insomnia, are often stress-related and so psychological counselling could also prove useful when medical intervention fails.

Text B

Lifestyle changes to improve sleep

Having difficulty sleeping? Here are some tips to ensure a good night's sleep:

- Eliminate caffeine from your diet. Caffeine is a stimulant and not conducive to sleep; so cut out coffee, tea and soft drinks.

- Learn to breathe deeply. Practise daily breathing exercises.

- De-stress your life. Try not to take work worries home with you. If something is bothering you and keeping you awake, write it down. The problem will not seem so big, afterwards.

- Before sleeping, take a warm bath so you feel fully relaxed before going to bed. Also, before going to sleep, try to read a good book so you can take your mind off any problems you may have that might keep you awake at night. Make sure the book is not too stimulating, however, as it will be more likely to keep you awake, than induce sleep.

For more information, contact: <u>info@health.org</u>

Text C

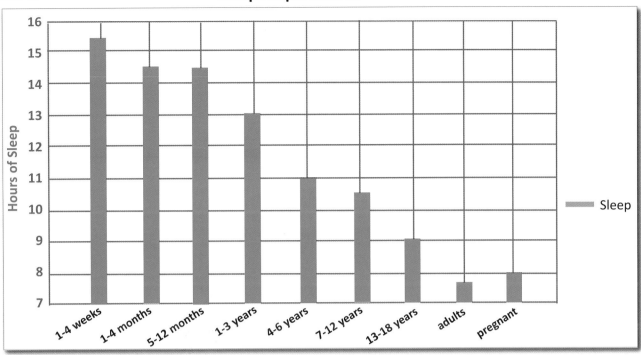

Sleep Requirements

Age	Additional Notes
1-4 weeks	Newborns are developing their internal biological clocks
1-4 months	Regular sleeping patterns begin and longer night sleeping
5-12 months	Important to establish regular sleeping patterns at this time
1-3 years	Naps remain important to sleep health
4-6 years	Naps will become shorter
7-12 years	Bedtime gets later
13-18 years	Teens may need more sleep
adults	Times will greatly vary
pregnant	More sleep and naps required

Text D

Strange sleeping patterns

The link between Napoleon, the late former UK Prime Minister, Margaret Thatcher, and Leonardo da Vinci is not immediately apparent. However, all fell within extreme ends of the sleeping spectrum. Margaret Thatcher famously got by on only 3 hours' sleep a night, whilst Napoleon dozed happily for up to 10 hours nightly. The most bizarre sleeping pattern of all, though, was exhibited by scientific genius and inventor, Leonardo da Vinci. His contributions to the world of technology and art made him an outstanding individual and so it seems fitting that Leonardo failed to conform to the normal sleeping habits of ordinary people, either.

Da Vinci exhibited a polyphasic sleep pattern, known as the Uberman sleep cycle. He slept for no more than a total of 2 hours in a 24-hour period, however his sleep consisted of 20-minute naps every 4 hours. Whilst this is undoubtedly unusual, he was by no means a unique case. What can be seen from all such vastly differing sleep patterns amongst these and ordinary individuals is that there is never one ideal sleeping pattern that suits everyone. Unusual sleeping patterns are not merely the province of geniuses and high achievers; lesser mortals, too, may require seemingly excessive or minimal amounts of sleep.

Test 5

Questions 21-25 (one mark per question)

Choose five statements from A-H below that are TRUE according to the information given in the texts above. **Write the letters of the TRUE statements on the lines below (in any order).**

21. ....

22. ....

23. ....

24. ....

25. ....

A	Only exceptional individuals tend to exhibit unusual sleeping patterns.
B	Eight hours' sleep is not always necessary for good health.
C	Environmental factors are not the only cause of sleeping disorders.
D	Physical illness may manifest itself as a sleeping disorder.
E	Medical intervention is necessary only in chronic sleeping disorders.
F	Naps are essential for adults and children, alike.
G	Hours spent sleeping diminish with age.
H	Psychological help should be sought first, in cases of insomnia.

Questions 26-30 (one mark per question)

The summary notes below contain information from the texts above. **Find a word or phrase from texts A-D to complete the missing information in gaps 26-30**. Write your answers on the lines below.

Summary notes

Sleeping disorders

Causes and cures

- Certain factors could lead to chronic sleep disorders e.g. **(26)**... .
- Stressful factors also can affect sleep e.g. work worries.
- Conditions like insomnia may benefit from non-medical intervention e.g. **(27)**.. .
- Many stress-related disorders can be relieved by relaxation techniques e.g. a warm bath/daily breathing exercises.

Sleeping patterns

- Teens differ in sleep patterns from younger children because they **(28)**.. .
- Pregnant women will also have different requirements e.g. more sleep/naps required.
- Children approaching their teens display a change in sleeping patterns as **(29)**.. .
- Some sleeping patterns, such as da Vinci's polyphasic sleep pattern, are **(30)**.. .

Task 3 – Reading into writing

Use the information from the four texts you have read to write a report (200-230 words) for a health blog. The topic of your report is what factors regulate sleeping patterns and what can be done in the case of irregular sleep.

You should plan your report **before** you start writing. Think about what you want to say and make some notes to help you in this box.

Planning notes

(No marks are given for these planning notes)

Now write your report of 200-230 words. Try to use your own words as far as possible - don't just copy sentences from the reading texts.

When you have finished your report, spend 2-3 minutes reading through what you have written. Make sure you have answered the task completely. Remember to check how you made use of the reading texts, as well as the language and organisation of your writing.

Task 4 – Extended writing

You have been discussing technology in your class. You have been asked to write an essay (200-230 words) giving your opinion on the topic: 'Technology, on the whole, has greatly improved our quality of life'. Do you agree?

You should plan your essay **before** you start writing. Think about what you want to say and make some notes to help you in this box:

Planning notes

(No marks are given for these planning notes)

Now write your essay of 200-230 words.

When you have finished your essay, spend 2-3 minutes reading through what you have written. Make sure you have answered the task completely. Remember to check the language and organisation of your writing.

Task 1 – Long reading

You are going to read about changing lifestyles and sleep patterns. Read the text below and answer the 15 questions that follow.

Paragraph 1

Many of us fret if we fail to get a good night's sleep; by that we mean 7-8 hours' uninterrupted shut-eye. Innumerable self-help books on how to improve sleep testify to the prevalence of sleeping disorders in modern society. Insomnia and disturbed sleep are in fact a lot more common than one might think. Indeed, sleep problems are so prevalent in the West that up to 30% of patients treated by GPs are believed to have problems stemming from sleep disturbance. However, recent research would seem to suggest that not only is a solid block of sleep unnecessary, but it may also be detrimental to our health. Tossing and turning in our beds at night trying to get back to sleep once awake, it appears, is actually going against our internal body rhythm.

Paragraph 2

Recent research on non-consolidated sleep has shown that humans didn't always sleep for 8 hours consecutively. Instead, our ancestors preferred to sleep an initial 3-4 hours, stay awake for a couple of hours, then sleep the same amount of time again until daybreak, this bimodal pattern of sleep occurring within a 12-hour time frame. Roger Ekrich, a historian from Virginia Tech University US, who conducted the research, supports his findings with historical evidence from sources as diverse as Homer's *Odyssey* to tribes indigenous to Nigeria. Within medical books, literature and diaries there is evidence, claims Ekrich, of bimodal sleep patterns which have now all but disappeared in modern society.

Paragraph 3

Interestingly, Ekrich's research appears to be supported by earlier scientific sleep experiments conducted in the 1990s, by psychiatrist, Thomas Wehr, former chief to the Clinical Psychobiology branch of the National Institute of Mental Health. Wehr found that subjects, placed in a darkened room for 14 hours a day for a month, naturally adopted a bimodal sleep pattern. The subjects would sleep for around 4 hours, awaken for a few hours, then return to sleep until morning. Dr Ekrich suggests that the pattern that Wehr's subjects fell into reveals how our bodies are designed to sleep. According to Ekrich's research, the bimodal sleep pattern, that is our natural sleeping rhythm, began to disappear around the turn of the 18th century. Such a pattern originated, Ekrich claims, amongst the aristocracy, catching on amongst the lower and middle classes until, 200 years later, the bimodal sleeping pattern had all but disappeared.

Paragraph 4

Changes in sleep patterns coincided with the advent of the Industrial Revolution. The mechanisation of life made people more aware of using time effectively. Also the introduction of electric lighting enabled people to stay up longer, later, thereby further disrupting natural sleeping patterns. People were no longer governed by the daylight hours, labouring from dawn to dusk. Electric lighting permitted people to work throughout the night, if so wished. Paris was the first major city in the world to light up its streets, followed soon afterwards by other major cities in the world. By the end of the 17th century, it was standard practice for Europeans to stay up at night. Prior to this period the night had belonged to criminals and other disreputable individuals and there was no obvious advantage for decent folks to be up and about during the night time.

Paragraph 5

Today, the idea that 8 hours' unbroken sleep is conducive to good health is so ingrained in our belief system that we panic when we wake up in the middle of the night and can't get back to sleep. According to Dr. Ekrich, what we should be doing instead is getting up, walking around for a couple of hours or working, then sleeping until daylight. Two periods of sleep are apparently far healthier than a consolidated 8-hour period of rest. It is not mandatory, however, to stay awake for the same time period each night; individuals vary in the time required to remain awake but the key, apparently, is to be consistent in sleep patterns. This research should come as a relief therefore to those who suffer from disturbed sleep. Ironically such individuals with 'sleep problems' probably have more natural sleep patterns than those of us enjoying 8 hours of uninterrupted sleep nightly.

Questions 1-5 (one mark per question)
The text on the previous page has 5 paragraphs (1-5). Choose the best title for each paragraph from A-F below and **write the letter (A-F) on the lines below**. There is one more title than you need.

1. Paragraph 1 ....

2. Paragraph 2 ....

3. Paragraph 3 ....

4. Paragraph 4 ....

5. Paragraph 5 ....

> A Practical advice
> B Normal habits are resumed
> C More harm than good
> D Inconclusive evidence
> E A historical explanation
> F Past proof

Questions 6-10 (one mark per question)
Choose the 5 statements from A-H below that are TRUE according to the information given in the text on the previous page. **Write the letters of the TRUE statements on the lines below (in any order).**

6. ....

7. ....

8. ....

9. ....

10. ....

> A Disrupted sleep has always been perceived as a problem, in the West.
> B Our ancestors benefited from 2 distinct periods of sleep.
> C Historical changes affected sleeping patterns.
> D Waking up during the night causes medical problems.
> E During night waking periods, individuals should be active.
> F Individuals need not strictly adhere to a 2-hour waking pattern in the night.
> G No scientific evidence exists to support Ekrich's theory.
> H Ekrich's theory is supported by both historical and scientific research.

Questions 11-15 (one mark per question)
Complete sentences 11-15 with a word, phrase or number from the text (maximum 3 words). **Write the word, phrase or number on the lines below.**

11. Many individuals mistakenly believe that their health issues are a result of ....

12. Ironically, a solid 8-hours' sleep is likely to .... to health.

13. Ekrich argues that .... suggests our ancestors adopted a bimodal sleeping pattern.

14. Further support for Ekrich's theory comes from the .... of Wehr.

15. The Industrial Revolution and electric lighting affected .... adversely.

Task 2 – Multi-text reading

In this section there are 4 short texts for you to read and 15 questions for you to answer.

Questions 16-20 (one mark per question)

Read questions 16-20 first and then read texts A, B, C and D below the questions. As you read each text, decide which text each question refers to. Choose one letter A, B, C or D and write it on the lines below. You can use any letter more than once.

Which text:

16. compares verbal and non-verbal communication?   ....

17. clarifies what body language is?   ....

18. identifies an error that people often make?   ....

19. acknowledges cultural differences in body language?   ....

20. provides information on body language in regular installments?   ....

Text A

Lewisham Group Intercultural Training: *Cultural Communication Skills for International Business Success*

Highly tailored and interactive blended learning solutions designed to provide international personnel, in every function, with the required skills, knowledge and tools to develop both general and culture specific intercultural business skills. In these days of increasing globalisation, employer and employee alike need to be informed of culture-appropriate behaviour and communication. We are living in an age where we need to be aware of a whole range of different cultures with whom we come into contact on a daily basis.

Our fully interactive courses explore the issues of working in an international environment, whether from the perspective of working with a specific culture, or whether you need to bring a specific skill into the global arena, such as 'Presenting to an International Audience' or 'Working in a Virtual Team'. We also offer a full range of intercultural communication 'Awareness and Competence' workshops centering on variations in cultural body language to maximise your global effectiveness. Our training solutions are targeted on matching your specific situational and strategic needs.

Text B

The employment blog

Wondering why you failed to get a job interview? You're not the only one. In fact, it is often something that you're not *saying* but *doing* that is to blame. Forget all those 'trick' questions that you prepared your answers for; the answers for that all-important interview and the ready responses that you had to hand to counter any difficult, probing questions about education, experience etc. No, what you need to be thinking about is how you sit, talk, your gestures and even the tone of voice you use! It's these non-verbal cues that make a potential employer decide to employ you or not.

Some potential employers state that they can size up an interviewee within just 30 seconds of their entering the interview room and that's before they even start talking! That's pretty alarming, when you think about it. The pressure is on to impress, almost instantaneously. Failure to do so will render whatever you say, however impressive, as totally irrelevant to any potential employer, thereafter. However, if you follow the weekly advice on this blog, you will find out how to win friends and influence people just by using body language! You will see dramatic changes in your working and personal life if you employ simple tactics that will make others see you in an entirely new light. It's something that you can't afford not to know! It will also serve to prevent you from unwittingly offending someone by using inappropriate body language.

Subscribe to this site and you won't be disappointed!

Text C

Forms of body language

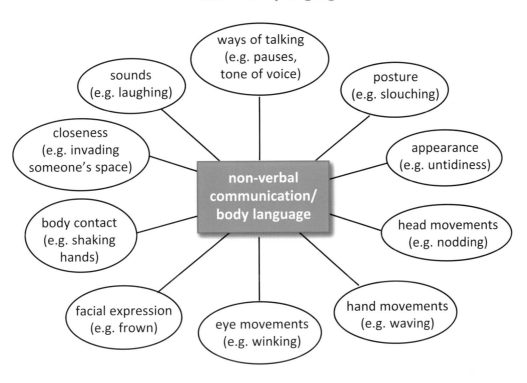

Text D

The scientific behavioural journal

Research indicates that non-verbal communication plays a far more prominent role in our everyday lives than verbal communication. Many people are simply unaware of how important body language is. If we better understood how our gestures and other forms of non-verbal communication were being interpreted by other people, we would definitely be more guarded in our body language.

Unwittingly, we may completely undermine whatever point we are trying to get across to an audience, by sending out non-verbal signals that contradict in some way what we are trying to convey. An everyday example of this is a politician, who whilst making election promises, continually touches his nose, which is a sure indication of lying, or maybe an interviewee who whilst boasting of skills or accomplishments fails to make eye contact with the interviewer or shifts about uncomfortably in his or her seat, indicating that they are not telling the complete truth.

In fact what we say accounts for only 7% of the overall impression that others have of us. Body language accounts for a staggering 55% of the impression others form of us, second in importance being the role played by the voice (38%), such as tone, modulation and pauses.

Given how important body language is, it is astounding that few practical courses exist to teach us about such a vital method of non-verbal communication, whilst emphasis is placed instead on verbal communication and the learning of new languages.

Test 6

Questions 21-25 (one mark per question)

Choose five statements from A-H below that are TRUE according to the information given in the texts above.
Write the letters of the TRUE statements on the lines below (in any order).

21. ………

22. ………

23. ………

24. ………

25. ………

A	We are usually fully aware of non-verbal cues we use, but don't exploit such knowledge.
B	Interviewees should pay more attention to what they say in interviews.
C	Courses run by the Lewisham Group can be structured to suit clients.
D	More than half of the information we convey to others is non-verbal.
E	Potential employers may focus more on a candidate's body language than their words.
F	The voice is just as important as body language in conveying information.
G	What we wear sends out a non-verbal message to others.
H	Even audible sounds we make, indicating emotion, constitute non-verbal communication.

Questions 26-30 (one mark per question)

The summary notes below contain information from the texts above. **Find a word or phrase from texts A-D to complete the missing information in gaps 26-30**. Write your answers on the lines below.

Summary notes

Non-verbal communication

Why it is necessary

• Knowing about another culture's body language can aid business and **(26)**………………………………………… .

• In certain situations e.g. **(27)**…………………………………………, many people would benefit from body language awareness.

• Being aware of body language can empower you socially e.g. win friends, influence people.

• In social situations, certain non-verbal behaviour e.g. inappropriate body language could potentially offend.

Types

• Body language, compared to verbal communication, has a significantly **(28)**………………………………………… .

• We convey messages just through our physical presence e.g. posture.

• **(29)**………………………………… place non-verbal emphasis on what we are saying e.g. head, hand movements.

• Not just our body but also our faces convey information e.g. **(30)**………………………………………… .

Task 3 – Reading into writing

Use the information from the four texts you have read to write an essay (200-230 words) for a health magazine. The topic of your essay is the importance of non-verbal communication.

You should plan your essay **before** you start writing. Think about what you want to say and make some notes to help you in this box.

Planning notes

(No marks are given for these planning notes)

Now write your essay of 200-230 words. Try to use your own words as far as possible - don't just copy sentences from the reading texts.

....

....

....

....

....

....

....

....

When you have finished your essay, spend 2-3 minutes reading through what you have written. Make sure you have answered the task completely. Remember to check how you made use of the reading texts, as well as the language and organisation of your writing.

Task 4 – Extended writing

You have been discussing in your class a film (or a book) that most of your classmates disliked. You have been asked by your teacher to write a review of this film/book (200-230 words) describing the plot, why you think that most of your classmates didn't like it and giving your own opinion.

You should plan your review **before** you start writing. Think about what you want to say and make some notes to help you in this box:

Planning notes

(No marks are given for these planning notes)

Now write your review of 200-230 words.

....

....

....

....

....

....

....

....

When you have finished your review, spend 2-3 minutes reading through what you have written. Make sure you have answered the task completely. Remember to check the language and organisation of your writing.